30 DAYS TO CRUSH CHAOS

30 DAYS TO CRUSH CHAOS

A Devotional for Finding Peace

Manny Arango

WATERBROOK

WaterBrook

An imprint of the Penguin Random House Christian Publishing Group, a division of
Penguin Random House LLC

1745 Broadway, New York, NY 10019

waterbrookmultnomah.com

penguinrandomhouse.com

Interior illustration: @ Spencer Fuller / Faceout Studio (dragon)

Some material is adapted from *Crushing Chaos* by Manny Arango, copyright © 2025 by
Manny Arango Ministries, Inc., published in the United States by WaterBrook, an imprint of
the Penguin Random House Christian Publishing Group, a division of
Penguin Random House LLC, in 2025.

Library of Congress Cataloging-in-Publication Data

Names: Arango, Manny, author.

Title: 30 days to crush chaos : a devotional for finding peace / Manny Arango.

Other titles: Thirty days to crush chaos

Description: First edition. | [Colorado Springs, CO] : WaterBrook, [2025] |
Includes bibliographical references.

Identifiers: LCCN 2024056957 | ISBN 9780593601655 (hardcover) | ISBN 9780593601662 (ebook)

Subjects: LCSH: Christian life—Prayers and devotions. | Christian life—Biblical teaching. |
Chaos (Christian theology)

Classification: LCC BS680.C47 A733 2025 | DDC 242/.4—dc23/eng/20250215

LC record available at https://lccn.loc.gov/2024056957

Printed in the United States of America on acid-free paper

1st Printing

First Edition

The authorized representative in the EU for product safety and compliance is
Penguin Random House Ireland, Morrison Chambers, 32 Nassau Street, Dublin D02 YH68,
Ireland. https://eu-contact.penguin.ie

BOOK TEAM: Editor: Drew Dixon • Production editor: Jessica Choi • Managing editor: Julia Wallace •
Production manager: Kevin Garcia • Copy editor: Tracey Moore • Proofreaders: Bailey Utecht,
Carrie Krause, Marissa Earl

Book design by Diane Hobbing

For details on special quantity discounts for bulk purchases, contact
specialmarketscms@penguinrandomhouse.com.

Contents

How to Use This Devotional

Hey! I'm glad you're here. Reaching out to you through these pages is a privilege. And I prayed for you as I wrote. Consider this an invitation to pray for me, too, as you read—I need it!

This thirty-day devotional coincides with my book *Crushing Chaos: Calm Your Storms. Order Your Life. Find Your Peace.* Each day of the devotional relates to a portion of the book—you'll find the corresponding chapter number(s) included with that day's devotional title. I recommend a couple different options for taking in both of these. One is to read a chapter of *Crushing Chaos* and then the related day (or days) here. Or, you could read the book all the way through first and then read one day of this devotional for thirty days straight. But don't beat yourself up if you miss a day or two or three. There is no wrong way to do it—the important thing is consistency. Find a rhythm of reading these that works for you.

I've set it up so this devotional is split into four weeks.

Each day, I highlight a Scripture verse related to the corresponding chapter(s) in my book, provide some devotional thoughts, and end with a couple of reflection questions for you to wrestle with. I've left you some space in case you want to journal your answers to the questions right here in this book. The very last part of each day is a short prayer prompt—it is easy to skip over this, but you will get a lot more out of this devotional if you don't. I want to challenge you to take a few minutes and pray, asking God to grow your trust in Him and help you apply what you've been learning about crushing Chaos.

I am so excited for you to encounter the Chaos-crushing God of the Bible in these pages. There is a whole world for us to discover and a totally, radically new way to see it. Let's do this together.

30 DAYS TO
CRUSH CHAOS

CHAOS
CHAPTER 1

In the beginning God created the heavens and the earth. Now the earth was formless and empty, darkness was over the surface of the deep, and the Spirit of God was hovering over the waters.

—GENESIS 1:1–2

"In the beginning..." When did you first hear those words that begin the Bible?

I grew up in church, so I heard that phrase maybe a thousand times or more before I started reading Genesis differently. I had read about God creating, and I believed it, but I was missing so much of the depth. After years in ministry, I circled back to Genesis because I was watching a trend in my congregation: Anxiety was on the rise. We were seeing fear and helplessness and panic attacks. I had preached dozens of messages about anxiety and panic. We had devoted prayer and ministry time specifically focusing on anxiety, but clearly, we hadn't cracked the code on the path to peace. Nothing had changed. We had no idea what we were doing wrong. Could anything be done about the chaos of anxiety? What would restore peace to our hearts?

Then I remembered that the creation account in Genesis has a whole lot to say about Chaos and that it describes the original state of creation as a deep, wild, raging ocean of Chaos. I wondered how the very first audience would have responded to this depiction, so I started looking in Scripture for the patterns, symbols, and repeated storylines they would have listened for. And the connections floored me. The creation story encompasses more than just the first two chapters of the Bible. God's work of creation echoes throughout the book of Genesis and the rest of the Old Testament, as well as throughout the Gospels and the rest of the New Testament. Once I started reading Genesis with the ancient context in mind, it became much more relevant to my life. It wasn't just a story anymore. These words, as old as they are, revealed something about my twenty-first-century heart.

Let's start with the first two verses in the Bible—today's passage. We're told that God is the creator of the earth and everything else, and then we zoom in on the earth itself to see that it was "formless and empty, darkness was over the surface of the deep, and the Spirit of God was hovering over the waters." Simply put, Scripture's first words declare that creation was a chaotic, untamed mess and that the Spirit of the Lord God was brooding over the surface of this barren, unintelligible, chaotic ocean abyss. Pretty epic visual, if you ask me.

Here's something that makes it even more epic—the ancient audience would have recognized the emptiness (or "wilderness" in some translations), the covering darkness, and the deep waters as symbols for Chaos. When hearing of the rushing waters of the great, unknowable deep, they would have felt the fear that such impenetrable darkness evokes. They would have recognized the challenge inherent in the creation story and wondered, *What does God do about that?* The world was uninhabitable. For anyone or anything to live or be planted in such a place, conquest would have to happen first.

You know what else is an untamed mess? We are. I am. Without God, the natural state of things is chaos, whether on the cosmic or personal level. We're messes. We're full of contradictions. Don't even get me started on our priorities. We don't even know what to want. We find ourselves doing things we know we shouldn't all the time. We're hurt by the chaotic choices other people make.

Disease, anxiety, abuse, poverty—they're all chaos. Sin is chaos.

What does your own chaos look like? Is it relational? Physical? Emotional? What chaos in your life leaves you feeling helpless, trapped, or anxious? How would you describe your experience of chaos to a friend who cared?

Whether or not it was your fault, it was never supposed

to be this way. Maybe you have become enveloped by your own chaos and wondered, like I have, *God, what could You do about this mess?* Even though we may find ourselves pondering that question, we have good reasons to hope.

Chaos was there at the beginning, and it has persisted throughout human history. Just grab any history book off the shelf, and in its pages you'll find that things have been chaotic for a long time. Most of us don't give the people who lived thousands of years ago enough credit; we have a bad habit of thinking our lives are more complicated than theirs. But they knew the same kinds of chaos that we do, and they longed for the chaos to be crushed. They wanted peace too. And Genesis—the story about the very first moments of the world—revealed the path they were looking for.

I wonder how many of us have rebuked anxiety but have yet to reject the forms of chaos that produce anxiety in our lives. The Bible provides a path out of Chaos, but it requires that we recover an ancient way of reading the Scriptures.

So, I invite you back to the beginning—either again or for the first time—to open Genesis and look for some symbols and signs we'll consider together. Maybe you've seen them before, or maybe you haven't. Either way, we're going to read the creation story carefully with ancient eyes because that perspective illuminates everything that comes afterward, all the way up to us, here and now. And we'll see that God knows exactly what to do with teeming, untamed chaos—in the world and in us.

Reflect

What forms of chaos are you experiencing in your life right now? How have you tried to handle them on your own?

_____

_____

_____

_____

When you think about reading Scripture with "ancient eyes," what excites or feels challenging to you? What new understanding do you hope to gain?

_____

_____

_____

_____

Pray

In prayer, call out to the Spirit of God, who hovers over your heart.

A WORLD OF CHAOS

This week, we're going to read the creation account together. Be on the lookout for patterns and connections you've never seen before. Ask God to give you eyes to see, ears to hear, and a heart to understand this story of the way He created our world. Ask for wisdom as we look at what our world was, what it became, and what God is doing in it now.

Order
CHAPTER 1

> God said, "Let there be a vault between
> the waters to separate water from water."
> So God made the vault and separated the
> water under the vault from the water above
> it. And it was so.
>
> —GENESIS 1:6–7

Yesterday, we established that God confronted Chaos with His work of creation, but not in the way we may have remembered or expected. In its original state, creation was a barren, unintelligible, chaotic wasteland. So, what did God do about the Chaos? I used to think that in creating the world, He brought peace—the same kind my congregation and I kept praying for when faced with an epidemic of anxiety. But when I looked at the first verses in Genesis again, I noticed something profound that often gets overlooked: God didn't bring peace to the Chaos; He brought Order.

Did you get that? God counters chaos not with peace

but with *order*. This makes all the difference. The Bible provides a path from chaos to order, and as I began to discover that path for myself and teach it to others, I started seeing less and less anxiety.

If we read through the creation story, we see that God was organizing and bringing order to the world. He began to separate, pull apart, gather, and bring structure to the chaos of creation. Let's look at the words God spoke in the first of today's verses, Genesis 1:6: "Let there be a vault between the waters to separate water from water."

What did God do? God *separated*. Just as He had separated light from darkness, ushering in the evening and morning, God ordered the waters by separating them, relegating them to their own spaces. The separated waters became the sea and the sky. God gathered the waters, uncovering dry ground, making the land and sea distinct.

The beginning of creation reveals a God who knows how to rearrange, organize, unclutter, clean, uncomplicate, simplify, and structure life. Again, God's solution for the Chaos found in Genesis wasn't to bring *peace*; it was to establish *Order*. Ironically, peace is always a natural byproduct once Order takes root in the cosmos, and I have discovered that God's strategy for responding to Chaos hasn't changed. Because the same sovereign Creator who pulled creation out of the chaos *then* wants to rescue our lives from chaos *now*.

Have you ever wondered why God doesn't usually solve our problems, heal us, or fix us instantaneously? He could—we know that. But He often doesn't. That's not His strategy when it comes to Chaos. Probably for the same reasons He gathered and separated and named creation, He works to bring Order to our hearts. God is patient. He's willing to work with us. He wants to crush the Chaos in our lives, but He wants to sow Order along the way. God is not impressed with the fast cure, because He knows that the slow, steady cure is more likely to take hold. I had been preaching about peace, essentially medicating pain and providing temporary quick fixes, instead of addressing the root problem. Anxiety was a symptom of pain that pointed to a deeper ailment—Chaos.

The good news is that there's a cure for Chaos, and that cure is Order. Whatever is troubling our souls may run deep, but it's still within God's reach. He absolutely knows how to handle it.

Sounds good, right? Well, the shift out of Chaos requires that we submit to God's idea of Order. And here's the part that not everybody likes: The Order to life that's revealed in the Scriptures doesn't necessarily consider our personal preferences.

Take sex for example. The Bible's vision: Sex goes *after* marriage, not before. Confusing this sequence will inevitably create absolute chaos, and that chaos will create abundant opportunities for anxiety to thrive. It doesn't matter how much we pray for peace—peace will never be permanent in the soul of the person who rejects God's Order.

Sequence is simply one element of Order. Authority is another. In the creation story, we see God implementing

His authority and Order. It's beautiful and rhythmic, almost musical—"Let there be; let there be; let there be." Our families, churches, and institutions can flourish only when they are well ordered according to the system of healthy authority God has established. This is one of the ways God creates Order and guards us from Chaos. Yet we've all found ourselves in conflict with God's Order at one time or another. What has that looked like for you? Sometimes, we don't want to submit to His authority. Or, at the very least, we want to be fixed quickly.

I think that's what people tend to expect from God when they think of Him creating the world "out of nothing." In those first verses of Genesis, we see a God who took His time. He wants to take His time with you too. He's steadfast and trustworthy, and He knows what He's doing. When we change our theology, everything else changes as a result. Once I saw God less as the One who created everything "out of nothing" and more as the One who meticulously untangled the cords of creation in Genesis, I began to realize that He had the power, plan, and patience to unravel the tangled ball of my complicated, chaotic life. I began to trust the slow plan and the steady process of discipleship that would bring more and more of His order into my life.

God will respond to the chaos in your life in His way—which involves ordering, separating, and gathering rather than instant fixes. I want you to start looking for this kind of work in your life and heart.

Reflect

What aspects of your life feel most out of order? Why?

_____

_____

_____

_____

How might your life be different if these aspects were more ordered and less chaotic?

_____

_____

_____

_____

Pray

In prayer, ask God for patience as you place your trust in Him and His Order.

Rest

CHAPTER 2

> By the seventh day God had finished the
> work he had been doing; so on the
> seventh day he rested from all his work.
> Then God blessed the seventh day and
> made it holy, because on it he rested from
> all the work of creating that he had done.
>
> —GENESIS 2:2–3

In the beginning, God countered Chaos with His divine Order, and He wants to do the same with our hearts. But why? What's His purpose in doing so? Again, the creation story in Genesis will point us in the right direction.

Today's verses tell us that on the seventh day Elohim *rested* from His work of organizing the world. For the ancient reader, this was the natural climax of the entire creation story. God's rest proved that the creation project had been a success and that the space had been sufficiently ordered.

Without context, it's easy to think of that seventh day of

creation as an admonition to go to church. And yes, that's extremely important. But from the ancients' perspective, this day signified God's triumph over Chaos. This was the part in the movie where the soundtrack crescendos and the tears well in your eyes—the hero is victorious. God did it. Ancient audiences knew that gods rested only once their temples were ordered and sanctified. Now God could rest. And by giving Himself rest, He's given us the ability to rest too.

Just before this moving scene, God created people and a garden called Eden for them to live in. We're told in Genesis 1:27,

> God created mankind in his own image,
>> in the image of God he created them;
>> male and female he created them.

God had created a temple for Himself, and He wanted us to live in it with Him forever. You probably remember about how long we bought into that plan. We'll talk more about this in later days, but Adam and Eve, the people in Eden, rebelled against the order God had set for them— they broke His only rule. Instead of the rest and order in the garden, they chose the chaos beyond it. Their disobedience was a betrayal of our primary function, the reason we were created.

Our primary function as humans is to reflect the image and likeness of almighty God and to order our lives according to the reality that we are image bearers. That is the predominant reason we were created. It is our central function and our chief end. It is of first importance and occupies the place of primary priority.

We unleash chaos when we

are ignorant of our true function,
rebel against our true function,
attempt to redefine our function.

And we rob ourselves of rest. Because *where* you rest will dictate *how* you rest.

You can't rest well when you're outside God's Order, when you're trying to make things up on your own.

If we fail to operate according to our function as image bearers, we get released from the temple we were designed to dwell in because we have not carried out the purpose we were placed there to fulfill. And whenever we try to make an alternative environment our home, we become restless and tired and burned out because we were designed only to rest in temples.

You weren't designed for chaos. You'll never enjoy true rest until you embrace your true function and come back to your true home. Because, again, *where* you rest will dictate *how* you rest.

When we refuse to submit to God's Order, we can't rest. Think about the way you're living. Are you able to rest, or are you restless? Are you wandering away from His Order, resisting His rules? Are you wondering, like Adam and Eve did, if God's way is actually the right way?

You'll never be at rest unless you become a place of rest for the One whose image you bear. Paul reminds us that this is the ultimate goal: to order our lives in such a way that we become resting places for the divine presence. He tells the church at Corinth in 1 Corinthians 6:19–20, "Do you not know that your bodies are temples of the Holy Spirit, who is in you, whom you have received from God? You are not your own; you were bought at a price. Therefore honor God with your bodies." This is the ultimate goal of those made in His image. Because *where* you rest will dictate *how* you rest. And God wants to rest in us.

That was His goal in creating the world and placing us in it. He didn't create us so He could be more powerful. His purpose wasn't to use us to meet His needs—He doesn't have any. Creating us gave Him a lot of joy. He moved the ocean out of the way, pulled the sky away from the sea, because He was thinking of you at *rest,* full of His presence. He wants you to receive that grace because that's why He created you.

Reflect

Be honest with yourself and with God as you answer the following question: Where do you rest? What does this look like?

_____

_____

_____

_____

What keeps you from resting in God? How might you redirect your resting this week?

_____

_____

_____

_____

Pray

In prayer, thank God for His rest and for His longing to rest in you.

Monsters
CHAPTER 3

> The LORD God took the man and put him in
> the Garden of Eden to work it and take
> care of it.
>
> —GENESIS 2:15

I grew up understanding that Adam and Eve ruined perfection. There's a sense in which that's true. But Genesis reveals something about the garden where Adam and Eve were placed: It wasn't complete.

Look at Genesis 2:15. Humanity was put in the garden "to work it and take care of it." Yes, like we learned yesterday, Adam and Eve were supposed to rest, and God rested *in them.* But God intended work and rest to exist in a rhythm. The garden wasn't meant to be a static place, the figures of Adam and Eve staying exactly where they were like pieces of felt on a board in a Sunday school classroom. They were going to create, explore, and work—they had things to do, a mission to accomplish. That was always part of God's plan. And diving into Genesis showed me what those "things to do" might look like. But first, let me share a shocking piece of information:

Did you know there are monsters in the Bible?

Genesis 1:21 says, "God created the great sea monsters" (NRSV)—a category of creature known as *tannin*. Whether they were being called "sea monsters" or "Leviathan" or any other name, the mention of these creatures would have caused the original audience to feel goose bumps. The *tannin* were synonymous with Chaos. The Israelites were very familiar with these creatures and undoubtedly would've known many of them by name. Today, we have some familiarity with the customs of countries and cultures that are not our own. Yet even without our hyper-connectedness, the peoples of thousands of years ago experienced cultural exchange. They knew one another's stories. Every single creation account in the ancient world included these *tannin*, so it's not shocking that they show up in Genesis.

So, back to what Adam and Eve were going to do in Eden . . . Could it have anything to do with clearing the world of these monsters, these fearsome *tannin*? I don't think that's a stretch. Humans contending with and defeating terrible monsters. Sound familiar? This narrative arc rings so deeply within us—just look at our fairy tales and superhero stories. We were made to fight the chaos. To subdue it. To bring peace. And even before sin became a part of human life, our will to win against chaos was woven into who we are.

The Chaos monsters in the cosmos prove that Adam

and Eve have work to do, chaos to tame, order to spread, and adversity to overcome. Their role as image bearers gives them function, but the presence of the *tannin* gives them work and mission. And the talking *tannin* in the garden means they must be wise, alert, and on guard. The Garden of Eden is not a vacation. There's chaos to conquer, a wilderness to subdue. Remember, the environment is good but not perfect. And the lingering Chaos in the cosmos gives Adam and Eve a task to set their hearts and minds to accomplish.

Yes, Eden was paradise, and the people in it were glorious. All told, the picture was, as God says Himself in Genesis 1:31, "very good." But here's the thing: It wouldn't have been paradise if there had been nothing for them to do. They were supposed to work the garden because that's what was best for them.

Have you ever lived through a time when you didn't have much direction? Maybe there was no rhythm to your day-to-day life. You were missing the element of "working the garden," whatever that might have looked like. If you've been there lately or you're there now, you're not alone. But I want you to know that one reason it's so difficult is that you were not made to languish. You're not supposed to be static. You're meant to be working the garden, fighting the monsters, contending with the chaos—all with God's help. You were created, like our first parents, to work in and take care of the place where God has put you.

This starts, of course, with tending to ourselves, with battling the chaos within us. You can't bring peace to the chaos in the outside world if you're not willing to take on the chaos inside you. Take a moment right now to consider your own soul. Let your mind wander, and see what you find—is it peace or chaos? Probably some of both. But the God who can tame Chaos monsters is on your side.

I want to give you a vision of the well-gardened soul, the kind you could find in a person who has been willing to step up to the internal battle and try, with God's help, to conquer the chaos within. A well-gardened soul is an ecosystem where all the members of the soul—mind, emotions (heart), and will—work in congruent harmony. Where one's mind agrees with one's heart. Where their spirit agrees with their flesh. Where their will agrees with the divine presence resting within them. Chaos of the soul happens when internal conflict and turmoil create unrest within a person.

We need more missional Christians who see themselves as gardeners. We've had preachers and evangelists who create converts but who aren't themselves healthy or whole. We need gardeners. Gardeners create disciples and cultivate greatness within others. They care more about health than growth because health inevitably leads to growth. Gardeners exemplify health and wholeness and plant the seeds of God's Order within the Chaos of our world. We need these men and women who have embraced the Order of God, have applied it to their own souls, have experienced the complete atonement of God, and are billboards of biblical *shalom*.

Reflect

Do you tend to care more about health or growth? Why?

_____

_____

_____

_____

How could you redirect your focus to spiritual health this week? What is one step you could take to do so?

_____

_____

_____

_____

Pray

In prayer, thank God that He has given us the gift of purpose—work to do in our own hearts and in the world.

Dragon
CHAPTER 4

> The serpent was more crafty than any of
> the wild animals the LORD God had made.
> He said to the woman, "Did God really say,
> 'You must not eat from any tree in the
> garden'?"
>
> —GENESIS 3:1

I have a problem with the way people today tend to envision stories from Scripture. We have this awful tendency to make things boring, palatable, understandable. We want things to fit nicely and neatly on a set of PowerPoint slides. But we can't really do that with these ancient stories. They aren't safe. They aren't tidy. They sometimes reveal things about us that we'd rather not know. When we're brave enough to look more closely, we find some scary and unsettling details. But it's worth it. And together, we're going to take a closer look at that moment in the garden when we were first tempted.

When most modern audiences read of humanity's temptation in the Garden of Eden, we imagine Satan as a small, slithering garden snake. The only issue with this is that it probably doesn't line up with what the Bible's original audience envisioned. Crawling on its belly is a wildly illogical punishment for a snake who's already doing so. Could the text of Genesis be begging modern readers to ask a question that would've been obvious to an ancient audience? I think so.

Let's unwrap that scene described in Genesis 3:1. What if "serpent" doesn't quite cut it without more context? Like we read yesterday, Adam and Eve were placed in Eden to work it and take care of it. What if, every now and again, something came to threaten the peace? What if this serpent was more of a dragon? A *tannin*? A beast? Maybe Adam and Eve even had experience with this type of situation. Maybe Eve was engaging with the monster to defeat it.

That is what we all are wired for. It is the common dream that drives our species. We all want to kill the beasts, slay the dragons, overcome the monsters, and restore peace and order to the temple of creation. We're all standing in front of our own trees of knowledge, facing off with our own beasts and trying our best to defeat them.

The Dragon lashes out at Eve, using some of his favorite weapons: deceit and doubt. "Did God really say . . . ?" he starts. The battle begins. They parry, back and forth, lies and rebuttals, the tree of knowledge in the background. For Eve, it may have started like other battles, other chaos-crushing work she's done in the garden. But the Dragon has something else in mind this time. He wears her down, playing on her desire for knowledge and growth—after all, she is a gardener. Genesis 3:5 records the false promise that lures her into defeat: "You will be like God, knowing good and evil."

Once the original audience found out that the dragon in the garden could speak, the debate would be over. Those freed nomads wandering around the desert would've heard Moses's creation story and made the connection that Adam and Eve were being tempted by a Chaos monster—which changes everything.

This means Adam and Eve were deceived by a Chaos monster and thus became partners in bringing Chaos into the cosmos. That was the endgame the Dragon—also known as Satan—had in mind. It was the blow that would separate humans from God. So often we simply conclude that Genesis 3 is the moment that sin entered our world, but I think it may be helpful to introduce some ancient language into our vocabulary. The ancients would've seen Genesis 3 as the moment that the untamable force of Chaos broke into our culture.

So, Satan was luring Adam and Eve into partnering with Chaos. Which means that Satan's Chaos had limits until humanity unleashed it into the cosmos. That we're the real monsters. That the monster in my mirror is a bigger threat than the monster under my bed. That Chaos is not only out in the cosmos but also taking up residence within us.

It means that we are the Chaos monsters.

And you want to know what's scarier than Leviathan? A world full of humans that have become the Chaos.

Humanity was safe so long as Chaos was external, in the cosmos. So long as it was outside us, it was okay. But once the Chaos got inside us, we became the monsters.

What a way to fall—from the ones keeping the garden to the ones needing to be kept out. But God didn't leave us there. We'll talk more about this later, but you'll see the theme of succumbing to temptation pop up over and over again as we read Genesis and other Old Testament stories. If anything, it should remind you that you aren't alone. But one day, that theme will be reversed. Can you think of the moment? Be looking for it. In the meantime, be reminded of this: Even when we fell to temptation, God kept looking after us. He devised a way to crush the Chaos, even after we let it enter our hearts.

This is one reason it is so important to keep looking to His Word—because we can't defeat Chaos on our own. We need His strength, His help, His words, His stories. The Bible beckons us back to Order:

Tame the beasts.

Defeat the monsters.

And crush the Chaos Dragon in the garden.

Reflect

Do you tend to think of yourself as wired to conquer chaos? Explain.

_____

_____

_____

_____

What is one way you will do battle with the chaos in your life this week? Why might it be important to ask God for strength in this battle?

_____

_____

_____

_____

Pray

In prayer, ask God for the faith to believe what He says.

Deep
CHAPTER 5

> Then I saw "a new heaven and a new
> earth," for the first heaven and the first
> earth had passed away, and there was no
> longer any sea.
>
> —REVELATION 21:1

Take another look at the final phrase of our verse today, which comes from the book of Revelation: "there was no longer any sea." It's something that is easy to pass over and that maybe doesn't register the first time through. In case you've never read Revelation before, I'll introduce it like this: It is a sweeping, soaring, and somewhat confusing vision that Jesus's beloved disciple, John, beheld while in exile. Revelation is the exclamation point at the end of the Bible, an assurance that everything will be well. Jesus Christ is the Lord of history, John tells us with absolutely wild imagery. (Talk about Chaos monsters!) Jesus Christ will make everything new—and, according to this verse, there will be no more sea. But what's wrong with the sea?

Does this mean no beaches in heaven? Does John have something against the ocean? He was exiled on an island, after all.

I have great hope that our desire for the seaside will indeed be fulfilled in heaven, even if we can't imagine exactly what it will look like. Why no sea in John's vision, though? We need to go back to Genesis to find out.

The sea is another ancient symbol for Chaos. The Hebrew word for the sea or "the deep" in Genesis 1:2 is *tehom*. The *tehom* and the *tannin* were interconnected realities in the ancient world. The Chaos monsters (oftentimes simply referred to as sea monsters) were the embodiment of Chaos in the minds of ancient readers and writers, but the sea was the realm of Chaos. What is the *tehom*? It's the home of the *tannin*. Leviathan is a monster of the deep, a monster of the *tehom*. The depths of the ocean are unknowable and full of danger. Do you see why this symbol resonated with the Israelites, especially since their own boats were small and their waters could be crossed only at great risk?

There's no better image for being overtaken by Chaos than that of drowning. You've likely heard people use the phrase "I'm drowning." Of course, most folks aren't literally drowning when they say this, but they feel like life is pulling them under. They have no control. They can't keep their heads above the chaos. And they know there's something lurking under it, waiting to destroy them.

What about you? Have you ever felt like you were

drowning? Do you feel that way right now? You weren't designed to live like this.

Living beyond your means. Drowning in debt.
Buying Christmas gifts for people you see once a year.
Making everyone happy.
Impressing neighbors you don't even know.
Sinking deeper and deeper into numbness and anxiety.

The Dragon convinces us that we can survive at depths he knows will crush us.

A number of us are drowning in the chaos of people pleasing. And some of us actually *are* drowning in the depths of sin.

Sin always convinces us that we have everything under control and can stop whenever we'd like. But the reality is that although at first we begin playing with sin, eventually sin will be the one playing with us. That's the chaos of sin. It drags you into the depths and drowns you. It overwhelms you. And before you know it, you've lost all control.

It started with you looking at a website. But now you're drowning in a porn addiction.
It started with one DM or text message. But now you're drowning in an affair.
It started with you downloading one app. But now you're drowning in gambling debt.

Sin deceives us into believing that we're in control of our own chaos, but the truth is that you cannot control the force of Chaos. Only God can control it, and only He can rescue you. You need a lifeguard far stronger than you to rescue you from the raging waters and the great deep.

If you're drowning in chaos, whether from sin or other people's expectations, God has a lifeline. The force of Chaos has been present since the very beginning, yet God has a proven track record of rescuing His creation from Chaos, and He can rescue you. This is how the creation account of Genesis begins—with God pulling creation out of the watery depths of Chaos. The Bible has wisdom to get you safely back to shore; we just need to interpret Scripture well to extract that wisdom.

Maybe that's why you're here for these thirty days—to get a fresh perspective on Scripture. And I hope, so far, you've found some of that. The Bible is not a self-help manual or a great podcast or even a compassionate friend. There's nothing wrong with those things. But none of them can get you back to shore, out of the sea of chaos, when you're in over your head. The Bible points us toward the One who has all control over the wild waters and dangerous depths of Chaos. Whether you're drowning in the chaos of people pleasing or in the chaos of sin, God's grace will pull you out of the depths of the *tehom* and rescue you from the undertow of the raging floodwaters.

The sea is so indistinguishably linked with Chaos and Leviathan that in Revelation, John simply tells his audience that Yahweh has finally re-created the heavens and the earth and now there's no more sea. For John and his audience, eternal paradise is a creation with no sea. Tell me that Chaos has been destroyed for good without telling me that Chaos has been destroyed for good. No more sea—no more Chaos.

No *tehom,* no possibility of being dragged under. No more Chaos. No more monsters lurking beneath the surface. Everything—yes, even that absolute impossibility you're thinking of—is well. The other shoe is *never* going to drop. Can you even imagine it?

Reflect

Name some ways you have sought to control the chaos in your life. Did your efforts work?

_____

_____

_____

_____

Why is it important to recognize that only God can conquer Chaos? How might you lean less on your own strength and more on His today?

_____

_____

_____

_____

Pray

In prayer, thank God for the new heaven and the new earth.

Day 7

Dark
CHAPTER 6

> Through him all things were made; without
> him nothing was made that has been
> made. In him was life, and that life was the
> light of all mankind. The light shines in the
> darkness, and the darkness has not
> overcome it.
>
> —JOHN 1:3–5

As long as we're here, challenging modern assumptions
about the biblical text together, let me offer this: Scripture
is a story. I bet you've heard that comparison before. But
Scripture is also like a song—it repeats. And those repetitions are important, each layer adding something significant, something different, some new way of hearing truth.
The lines of the Bible dwell on the same idea using different imagery.

So far, we've talked about a few different symbols for
Chaos: the deep and the monsters. There are more symbols for Chaos, and each one helps us deepen our under-

standing of the others. Can you guess what symbol we're looking at today, based on our passage from the opening lines of the gospel of John?

It's not shocking to me that the Bible equates darkness with chaos and that the chaos of Genesis 1:2 isn't fully encapsulated by the sea or the raging flood; it also includes the darkness of the wilderness:

> The earth was *without form and void (tohu va-vohu)*, and *darkness (hosek)* was over the face of *the deep (tehom)*. And the Spirit of God was hovering over the face of *the waters (mayim)*. (ESV)

Darkness was over the deep; nothing could be known or seen anywhere, above or below, except by God. And that darkness would be overcome—or crushed—by God's light during creation. Of course, it came rushing back the moment Adam and Eve left the garden. They'd never been afraid of anything. But in the course of one terrible day, they felt shame before God, and I wonder if they felt afraid of the dark that night for the very first time.

Darkness is a perfect metaphor for chaos. How can you choose a path if you can't see? You'll stumble. The longer I'm in ministry, the more I watch people walk straight into all kinds of chaos that end up bringing unnecessary pain into their lives. I've witnessed people walk straight into adultery, addiction, debt, and toxic relationships. It's like they couldn't see what they were walking directly toward.

I can't count how many times I've said to a couple, "These behavioral patterns will lead straight to a divorce. That is the path you're on." I can see how they're five years away from a divorce because of the road they're traveling down, but they're blind to it. They're living in darkness.

What about you? Do you ever feel like you're living in darkness? Do you keep falling into certain patterns, habits, or behaviors that leave you blindly stumbling around? Do you ever find yourself desperately wishing that someone could turn on the light? Take courage. It doesn't have to be this way. There is a way out of the chaos of the overpowering darkness.

When I was twenty-two years old, my pastor at the time gave me the most succinct definition for wisdom I've ever heard. We were at a restaurant called Not Your Average Joe's, and I ordered the mustard-crusted chicken. This moment was over fifteen years ago, yet it's just as vivid in my mind as mental snapshots from last week. Pastor Matt looked at me and said, "Manny, do you know what wisdom is?" I shook my head no. And he responded, "Wisdom is foresight."

Wisdom is *foresight*. The ability to make decisions based on a vision of the future as opposed to the feelings of today. Wisdom is the ability to see around the corner. Wisdom prevents us from making shortsighted decisions.

Foresight.

God established light to subdue the chaos of darkness because everything that brings life grows in the light. And everything that multiplies chaos grows in the darkness. Have you ever felt so ashamed of some sin, suffering, or need that you just didn't tell anyone? How did that go for you? Did its weight diminish, or did it increase? I'd feel pretty safe guessing that it increased. Well, there's a reason for that. The primary way to feel worse about something and give it more power is to never tell a soul, to never confess, to think, *This is so terrible that I can't tell anyone.* By leaving it—whatever it is—under the cover of darkness, you're crafting the perfect environment for it to flourish. Maybe you don't do it intentionally, but this is the reality of the chaos of darkness.

Lies and shame.
Fear and depression.
Sin and secrets.
All of these grow in the dark.

Chaos multiplies in the darkness.

So what is God's solution for darkness? You guessed it. Light. Truth. Wisdom.

If you're hiding in the chaos of darkness, how can you bring your situation into the light? How can you bring it to Christ and, trusting in His guidance, reach out for the help you need? I take great comfort in John's words about Jesus in our passage for today: "Through him all things were made." This means that Jesus was there at the beginning. He—along with His Father and the Spirit—

dispelled the darkness. As John says, "The light shines in the darkness, and the darkness has not overcome it." Anyone who has felt overcome by darkness can rest assured of this: Christ will overcome it. Darkness cannot stand against Him. Because He is the one who crushes Chaos. He brings light and truth and wisdom. At last, we can see where we're going—but even more importantly, we can see *Him*.

Reflect

What areas of your life have you been keeping in darkness? How might bringing them into the light change things for you?

_____

_____

_____

_____

When you think about wisdom as foresight, what current decisions or patterns in your life do you need to reconsider? What future consequences might you be closing your eyes to?

_____

_____

Pray

In prayer, ask God for the courage to step forward into His light.

Desert
CHAPTER 7

> I looked on the earth, and lo, it was waste
>   and void;
>   and to the heavens, and they had no light.
> —JEREMIAH 4:23, NRSV

Let's recount the Chaos symbols we've encountered thus far: the monsters, the deep, and the darkness. All of these are unforgiving, and all would have brought a shiver to the original audience. Today, we're talking about the final Chaos symbol used in Genesis 1:2—the desert. It's the Hebrew phrase *tohu va-vohu,* translated as "waste and void" in today's verse out of Jeremiah.

To me, the darkness and the desert are somewhat distinct from the sea because it's obvious that humans cannot live in the sea. It is incompatible with human life—we would be dragged under and drowned. However, humans *can* live in the wilderness. And humans *can* live in darkness. Which makes the dark desert wilderness an exceptionally interesting realm of Chaos throughout the biblical narrative. There's a natural temptation to make the desert or darkness our home. We can survive in the darkness and we can survive in the desert, but these are not ideal environments for humanity.

Do you ever look around and see the ways that your environment hampers your growth? (I'm not talking about wanting a nicer house.) Do you ever feel deep loneliness, have difficulty connecting with the people around you, or think that maybe you could flourish somewhere far away? Perhaps you've struggled to settle into your surroundings. Maybe no matter how many friends you make, you still experience loneliness and stifled hopes. But here's the thing: Earth should feel a little strange to you because *this is not your home.*

The Dragon has convinced most of us that the desert wilderness we're living in is really a garden. He works overtime with his primary weapon—lies—to make chaos look appealing. "Is it really so bad?" he asks us. There are trees. There's fruit. There are rivers. Garden spaces and wilderness spaces share so much in common. So, we compromise and settle—out in the wilderness—and we lie to and convince ourselves that the desert is a suitable home for our souls. All the while, the Dragon whispers that it's more than good enough *and* that we don't deserve any of it. He tries to have it both ways. He's an excellent liar, remember?

How have Satan and his lies influenced you? Has he unleashed the same words on you that he did on Adam and Eve: "Did God really say . . . ?" What has that felt like? What did he manage to convince you was fine, even though it had the marks of chaos all over it? Maybe it was a relationship, a belief, or a situation you felt like you couldn't leave. For whatever reason, he lured you into being comfortable in the chaos. It's easy to mistake coping and surviving with conquering and thriving.

So many of us make this mistake. Our ability to cope with chaos has evolved into the cultural codes we live by. We're almost incentivized to remain in dysfunction because returning to the Order of the garden will require that we unlearn the coping mechanisms that have now calcified into habitual patterns.

Friend, God created you to thrive. And I'm not talking about getting everything you want. I'm talking about the peace of submitting yourself to His Order, of finding your place in His kingdom. You don't have to be content with chaos. You don't have to try to be okay with all these things that are not okay.

There was a time when my wife and I were watching wilderness-survival reality shows on TV, and I just want to point out a simple truth: When we talk about living in the wilderness, we describe that reality as *survival*. Some of the wilderness experts would build elaborate forts and set up complicated apparatuses and systems for cooking food, washing clothes, and guarding against wild animals. But it doesn't matter how fancy the makeshift shelter or how elaborate the system for catching food—it is still survival. I have been thoroughly impressed by some of those wilderness experts, but it's still *survival.* There is no thriving in the desert or flourishing in the wilderness. There are only short-term wins and long-term ramifications when we attempt to live in survival mode permanently.

We see examples in Scripture of humans trying to survive in the chaos. Think of the Israelites—the people of God who had been held in captivity in Egypt for hundreds of years. Moses led them out of Egypt, and they were headed for the land God promised them. But they got stuck in the desert, and not for a short time. They didn't want to submit themselves to God's rules. (Does that sound familiar?) God led the people of Israel out into the desert for a purpose and a season. They were never meant to remain in the chaos for forty years. However, the chaos of Egypt had forced them to adopt coping mechanisms that kept them stuck in the desert way longer than originally planned.

What about you—have you wound up in a place of chaos for longer than you intended? Maybe you have ways of making yourself comfortable in that spot. *It's just for a time,* you tell yourself, without any real plan for moving forward. You have no real notion to reach out to God or submit to His plan. Have you perhaps forgotten what your destination is supposed to be?

The account of the Israelites is just a foretaste of how humans and chaos interplay. There's so much to discover together. As we leave the dramatic scene of creation, let's see what other patterns, repetitions, and stories Scripture holds for us in other Genesis narratives and the rest of the New Testament.

But first, let's recap what we've covered so far. This will help as we go further together:

Order is rest. Temples. Image bearers. Gardens. Light. Wisdom. Life.

Chaos is wandering. Dragons. Beasts. Sea. Wilderness. Desert. Darkness. Death.

Reflect

What aspects of your life feel more like "survival mode" than thriving? How might God be calling you to move beyond just surviving?

_____

_____

_____

_____

When have you settled for chaos because it felt familiar or "good enough"? What keeps you from seeking God's better plan?

_____

_____

_____

_____

Pray

In prayer, ask God to help you remember the kind of world you were created for.

WEEK 2

TAMING THE BEAST

In this past week, we've seen how God deals with Chaos in the cosmos. He has incredible power over it and orders it to stay within certain bounds. Now we'll spend a week dwelling on how God deals with the chaos in us. To that end, we're going to meet (or re-meet) some Genesis characters who will help us see what God's redemptive works look like in us.

Day 9

Cain
CHAPTER 8

> If you do what is right, will you not be
> accepted? But if you do not do what is
> right, sin is crouching at your door; it
> desires to have you, but you must rule
> over it.
>
> —GENESIS 4:7

When I dove back into Genesis to learn what could be done about chaos, I noticed when things took an incredibly personal turn. The external chaos in the world is embodied by depth, darkness, and desert wasteland. But so much of the chaos we experience wells up from within. Our interior landscape can be just as bleak and terrifying as the scenes from the first lines of Genesis.

That's not how we started—we were part of a "very good," orderly creation (Genesis 1:31). The chaos inside us results from the curse God pronounced after we sinned. When the Chaos Dragon stood before Adam and Eve and deceived them into becoming hosts of Chaos, they lost what was most precious to them—God's ideal design for their humanity. In trying to be their own gods, they became beasts of impulse and instinct, and the remainder of Genesis begs us to ask this question:

What does it mean to be truly human?

When we find the answer to that question, we find the key to establishing Order and conquering Chaos. By recovering our humanity, we recover Order. But by continuing to live as beasts, we multiply Chaos. So, let's dive further into Genesis and find out how to be truly human by slaying the beasts living within us and taming the Chaos that surrounds us.

After Adam and Eve succumbed to the trickery of the Dragon, all three of them—man, woman, Dragon—were given specific curses. Now Adam must work hard to bring food from the ground. He must sweat. The work in the garden that was inherently joyful has been replaced by the work in the field that must be done but is not necessarily joyful. Eve must labor and birth children through pain. And the Dragon? He's going to be crushed. Genesis 3:14 reads, "Cursed are you above all livestock and above all beasts of the field" (ESV).

Genesis 2:19 in the ESV tells us that "out of the ground the LORD God had formed every beast of the field." And then verse 20 says that "the man gave names to all livestock and to the birds of the heavens and to every beast of the field" (ESV).

"Every beast of the field"—that precise phrasing is important. Not the beasts from the soil or the beasts from the ground.

Nope. Beasts of the field.

Genesis 3:1 says, "The serpent was more crafty than any other *beast of the field* that the Lord God had made" (esv). The Bible wants us to meld these images together in our minds—beasts and fields—so that we cannot see one without the other.

The Bible leaves us breadcrumbs to follow and symbols to interpret. God loves to establish patterns in His Word so that when a pattern gets broken, it'll grab our attention. Let's step into the story of Adam and Eve's children to see what happens when the Chaos curse is inherited.

Chaos infiltrates the order of Adam and Eve's family. They have two sons: Cain, then Abel. Abel's the second son, see? Yet when the two sons bring offerings to the Lord, God looks with favor on Abel's sacrifice of animal fat but not so on Cain's sacrifice of fruit from his harvest.

Then things get ugly. Genesis 4:8 tells us that "Cain said to his brother Abel, 'Let's go out to the field.' " And then . . . Cain kills him. God praises Abel, and Cain murders him for it. It's exactly the kind of Chaos disorder that happens—although usually to a lesser degree—in families all the time. Cain couldn't accept the way God dealt out blessings, so he took matters into his own hands. I wish it didn't sound so familiar to me.

Genesis teaches us that it is very easy for humans to slip into beast mode and begin to exhibit animal-like behavior.

You allow the beast to take you into the field and rob you of your humanity

> every time your temper gets the best of you,
> every time your lusts and your passions rule you,
> every time your instincts overtake your intentions,
> every time your primal urges aren't conquered,
> every time gossip and negativity erupt from your heart and flow from your lips.

Let me ask you some hard questions regarding your humanity: Do you practice Sabbath, or has your work turned you into a restless beast? Are you a workhorse, or are you a human?

Before the shame spiral hits here, though, I want to remind you that God knows how to turn beasts back into humans. It is one of His specialties. And there is nothing so beastly about you that God cannot help you reclaim your humanity. Cain does arguably one of the worst things a person can do—he kills his own brother. God doesn't strike him dead then and there. Cain has to leave, but God does not cast him off forever. I hear God saying these words from Genesis 4:7 to Cain firmly but gently: "Sin is crouching at your door; it desires to have you, but you must rule over it."

Just as God reminded Cain, I want to emphasize that you are not a beast. You were created to rule. You were created to master yourself. You were created to exercise self-control. You were created to rule over your heart and mind instead of letting them rule over you. You were created to overcome temptation. You were created in the image of God to conquer the beasts and crush the Chaos.

Reflect

In what areas of your life do you feel God calling you from "beast mode" back to humanity? What steps could you take toward that change?

_____

_____

_____

_____

When have you experienced God's patient work of bringing Order to your life? How did that experience give you hope?

_____

_____

_____

_____

Pray

In prayer, thank God that His desire is to redeem you.

Abraham
CHAPTER 9

> Some time later God tested Abraham. He said to him, "Abraham!"
>
> "Here I am," he replied.
>
> Then God said, "Take your son, your only son, whom you love—Isaac—and go to the region of Moriah. Sacrifice him there as a burnt offering on a mountain I will show you."
>
> —GENESIS 22:1–2

How does God turn us, beasts of the field that we become, back into people again? How does He re-humanize us?

Well, the process is never easy, but I doubt that you were expecting it to be. Let's continue working through the lineage in Genesis, our human history of beastliness. We're going to skip some important parts at the moment, but stay with me. We'll come back around to the great Flood in the third week of this devotional. So, beyond Noah and after the tower of Babel, we come to Abraham.

You might remember a song about Abraham from your childhood Sunday school days—*Father Abraham had many sons . . .* Just me? Sorry. Well, the tune of Abraham's life is a lot less catchy than the song. There are some serious moments of dissonance. He sometimes acts more like a beast than a human.

God promises Abraham and his wife, Sarah, a son, but they wait a long time for the fulfillment of that promise. In the meantime, they decide—together—that the best way to make sure God's promise comes true is to have Abraham sleep with Sarah's maidservant, Hagar. (Sometimes Scripture sounds like a soap opera. But this really happened.) The son born out of their decision is called Ishmael.

Despite all that, God still delivers on His promise to give Abraham and Sarah a son of their own. They're old. Past old—they're ancient. They were old when God called Abraham in the first place. But Sarah finally becomes pregnant and has a son named Isaac.

However, their own solution for their infertility has created a new problem. God miraculously solved the childlessness issue in His time, but now they have to deal with the problem their preemptive solution made. A foolish solution causing a new problem—does that sound familiar to you? It definitely sounds more like my life than I want to admit. So, Sarah and Abraham decide to do something about Ishmael and his mother. They throw them out into the wild—where the beasts live.

Since the Bible uses looping images and repetition to show us what's important, we should pay attention because the image of the human-beast hybrid is officially looping and repeating. Remember the pattern.

If the son of the Serpent is a predator, the son of the woman must get offered as prey. Is there anywhere in the narrative where Ishmael's brother, Isaac, gets offered as a sacrifice? Yes—yes, there is. Look at today's verses.

I think Isaac knew exactly what was happening by the time they got to the top of the mountain, by the way. There are pictures that show Abraham with a little boy, but the chronology of Genesis indicates that Isaac was already a teenager or young man.* This is a picture of Jesus and the Father. This is a foreshadowing of Gethsemane. The Father willed the sacrifice to occur, but the Son had to be willing to do it *together* for the Cross to be just and not cruel.

We all know the end of the story. The Angel of the Lord calls to Abraham from heaven and forbids him to kill Isaac. This was just a test—and all parties have passed. Abraham sacrifices a ram in Isaac's place, and everyone descends the mountain and goes to see a therapist. LOL.

---

* "How Old Was Isaac When Abraham Almost Sacrificed Him?," Got Questions, accessed November 27, 2024, www.gotquestions.org/how-old-was-Isaac.html.

Cain and Ishmael were the offspring of the Serpent. Abel and Isaac were the offspring of Eve. A pattern is emerging.

Abel's blood was spilled and sacrificed.
Abel kept flocks that he freely sacrificed to God.
Abel, the son of Eve, foreshadows Jesus—the ultimate
son of Eve.

Isaac was placed on the altar as a sacrifice to God.
Isaac was replaced at the last minute by a ram caught
in a thicket.
Isaac, another son of Eve, foreshadows Jesus—the ultimate son of Eve.

Abel and Isaac have defeated the Beast by laying down their lives.

Sometimes the Bible shows us how humans lose their humanity and chronicles their descent into animal-like tendencies. But we're not beyond redemption. God is in the business of not only ordering our world but also ordering us. He is in the business of taking broken humans like us and making us whole.

It's easy to be impressed by singular moments of transformation. However, each climactic moment of change was preceded by a journey where the wise and patient God of the Bible worked behind the scenes to guide the person down the road of redemption.

The transformation that God set in motion for Abraham is God's plan for you. He wants to heal you, make you whole, make you human again. And He wants to move in and through the circumstances you find yourself in to do it. He can move through your mistakes. He can move through grief and despair. He wants to bring wholeness to the things in your life that are broken.

Yes, the second time—or the millionth time—God offers us the chance to become human again, it's hard to open our hands and offer our lives. It's hard to leave our shame in the past and step forward into His plan. But with God's help, we can do it.

Reflect

What difficult second chances has God given you? How did those opportunities help reshape your faith?

When have you seen God's redemptive work happen slowly in your life? What fruit came from that patient process?

_____

_____

Pray

In prayer, ask God for the strength to accept His redemption.

The Twins
CHAPTER 9 AGAIN

> I will put enmity
>> between you and the woman,
>> and between your offspring and hers;
> he will crush your head,
>> and you will strike his heel.
>
> —GENESIS 3:15

After going through all that trauma with his own dad, Isaac probably knew better, right? He, at least, must have had more warning about the bad patterns that people can fall into, the flaws that can seep into families and threaten to topple them. Right?

You probably already know where I'm going with this. Unfortunately, Isaac had his own share of family problems. He finally got down off the mountain (and out of therapy) and married a woman named Rebekah. They hoped for children and believed God's promise to give

Abraham thousands of descendants. One of their children would receive the blessing Abraham had given to Isaac. Isaac and Rebekah had twin boys, and the details should immediately grab our attention. Genesis 25:25 tells us, "The first to come out was red, and his whole body was like a hairy garment; so, they named him Esau." Esau was born as a red, furry beast. And get this: Verse 27 says, "Esau was a skillful hunter, a man of the field" (ESV).

The Bible shows. It rarely tells. This is why it's so essential to learn the cues that the original audience would have been attuned to, even if we're coming to Scripture for practical and personal reasons. What is the Bible showing us? What symbols, patterns, and pieces of information are significant? I can tell you this: There's a whole world to discover—not just in Genesis but in the other books of Scripture as well. It's important not only to find teachers whom we trust but also to ask God for wisdom. This is His Word. He wants us to understand it. When we come before Him humbly, asking for help, He's not going to fail us.

Back to the moment at hand. The description in Genesis 25 is how the Bible communicates that Esau is the offspring of the Serpent. And beasts don't handle being hungry very well, which is why fasting will become one of the ultimate marks of practicing humanity throughout the Scriptures. Animals are obedient to their appetites. Humans are not enslaved by their stomachs but obedient to God.

So, we know the pattern. If Esau is the offspring of the

Serpent, his twin brother, Jacob, must be the offspring of the woman, right? Not so fast. If there's one thing the Bible loves more than creating a pattern, it's breaking the pattern. When Genesis 25:26 recounts Jacob's birth, we get a suspicious detail. It says, "After this, his brother came out, with his hand grasping Esau's heel; so he was named Jacob." The Hebrew word for "heel"* in this verse is also used in Genesis 3:15, where the Serpent is cursed. There, God promises that the ultimate son of Eve will crush the Beast's head but that the Serpent "will strike his heel." The crafty Dragon turned Serpent is a heel striker, and Jacob is a heel grabber.

We've read the other stories of this lineage in Genesis, and we've seen pairs before: Cain and Abel. Ishmael and Isaac. Now Esau and Jacob. They're *twins,* for crying out loud. This has to be another "beast and human" pair. One thing doesn't add up, though: Esau—the "beast"—is the older brother. Isaac has only one blessing to bestow, and he's planning to give it to Esau. The lineage is supposed to carry on through the blessed brother.

But the twins' mother isn't very happy about this. Apparently, Rebekah's favorite child is the twin who looks less like an animal, and she wants him to get the blessing. So, she comes up with a plan: Jacob will put hair on his arms and pretend to be Esau. Isaac, who is old at this point

---

* *Lexham Research Lexicon of the Hebrew Bible,* ed. Rick Brannan (Bellingham, Wash.: Lexham, 2020), s.v. "*aqeb.*"

in the story, won't be able to tell the difference because he can't see. We've already seen what happens when parents try to sort out the inheritance on their own (remember Ishmael?), and things take a similarly difficult turn in this story.

Let's put on our "original audience" glasses for a moment: Jacob and Rebekah go forward with their trick. And when Jacob puts on Esau's garments and Rebekah places the goatskins on his hands, it's a confirmation that Jacob, like his brother, is a beast. This is the moment where all hope for Jacob being a son of Eve is seemingly lost. Both young men are sons of the Serpent. Both are beasts.

But wait a minute! What about the redemption? What about the story of Jacob's birth? Isn't he supposed to be able to defeat the Serpent?

The Bible loves establishing patterns and then breaking them to get our attention. With Jacob and Esau, we have a plot twist. It seems the Serpent has won. But God is never in a catch-22, so He launches a plan to restore Jacob's humanity—and to ultimately transform him into a son of Eve named Israel.

I love the story of what happens to this heel-grabbing trickster. Jacob's story gives me hope—not just for myself but for all of us. I read it and hear it as a testimony that God can redeem *anyone.*

Reflect

How has God broken patterns of chaos in your family story? What healing have you witnessed?

_____

_____

_____

_____

When have you felt stuck in old patterns but seen God show up anyway? What did that teach you about His faithfulness?

_____

_____

_____

_____

Pray

In prayer, ask God to open your eyes, ears, and heart to the truth in His Word.

Jacob
CHAPTER 10

> I am with you and will watch over you
> wherever you go, and I will bring you back
> to this land. I will not leave you until I have
> done what I have promised you.
>
> —GENESIS 28:15

After such a beastly trick (sorry, couldn't help myself), Jacob follows his instincts. That heel grabber takes the blessing and runs for his life. Esau's a great hunter, remember? He wouldn't have too much trouble killing someone like Jacob. So, the younger twin runs away in the hope that his uncle Laban can provide him with refuge and the comfort of family. As a fugitive and foreigner, Jacob stops for the night and has a dream while lying in the middle of a town named Luz in the middle of nowhere. He's done absolutely nothing to deserve a divine visitation. Yet that's exactly what happens, because the grace of God often shows up when we least expect it and least deserve it.

The Bible tells us that "taking one of the stones there,

[Jacob] put it under his head and lay down to sleep. He had a dream in which he saw a stairway resting on the earth, with its top reaching to heaven, and the angels of God were ascending and descending on it" (Genesis 28:11–12). With a rock for a pillow, Jacob lies down under the stars and dreams of a ladder that connects heaven and earth. Angels are ascending and descending on this cosmic escalator, and then God promises Jacob that He won't forsake him, that his descendants will be great, and that he'll possess the land (verses 13–15).

Look at our verse for the day again. This is the end of God's speech to Jacob as he's lying there, cast away from his family, alone in the wilderness, sleeping on a rock: "I am with you and will watch over you wherever you go." God's faithfulness is not dependent on our faithfulness. He watches over us, even when we run away.

God was showing Jacob the same thing we all need to see to have hope—Jesus. The way that God showed Jacob isn't the way that all of us see Jesus, though. We don't all get this grand vision, the flash of insight, or the angels everywhere. God's voice may seem smaller to us than it did to Jacob, but it's always as persistent.

So, let's look at Jacob's encounter together. Jacob sees a vision, not just for himself but also for an entire family dedicated to being a portal for the divine presence to invade earth. And that family will turn into a tribe and then ultimately a nation—called to be a ladder that connects God with the nations of the earth. This is the message echoed through the rest of Scripture.

Jacob's vision reminds me that even though God starts small, He starts strong.

How did God recover Jacob's humanity even though he was a snake? In the same way He recovers our humanity: by showing us the ideal human. Jesus. The comprehensive model for this new way of being human in the world.

Jacob saw Jesus. And a true vision of Jesus changes everything.

Would Jacob build another tower or build a temple?

Will we build towers of Babel or temples of the Holy Spirit?

Will we build bridges for God or attempt to build towers to reach God?

Each represents a very different way of being human.

Jacob sees a vision of the kind of human God has called him to be. He leaves Luz knowing that he is called to be not a heel grabber but a ladder that Yahweh can use to deliver grace and shalom to humanity.

You may have heard people call Jesus a bridge builder—Jacob's vision brings a whole new dimension to that. We're called to leave our heel-grabbing ways and be like Jesus. God is a great redeemer and reconciler. He wants to bridge the gap between things that seem too disparate to reconnect, and He wants us to be ladders as well. How is God calling you to be a ladder in your own life? What contradiction is He calling you to help reconcile? What does He want you to unravel or unfold? What grudge does He want you to release? How can you stand in the middle for others, the way Jesus has done for you? God wants us to reach toward one another, not grasp for things we think we can't live without.

At this point, Jacob could've turned around and acted like the priest God had called him to be by returning home and reconciling with his brother, since reconciliation and atonement are the main functions of being a priest. I like quick fixes, too, so I wish I could tell you that Jacob did this, immediately acting on the vision he saw. But he didn't. Yet God—the separating, drawing-out, pushing-apart, ordering God of the universe—was willing to wait until Jacob was ready.

I know this sounds kind of odd, but I find it helpful too. Even though Jacob had a "blinded by the light" vision, he didn't turn everything around right then and there. He still had things to untangle, and he'd bear the consequences of them. Boy oh boy, does Genesis have a lot to say about consequences and long roads. But it also has a lot to say about redemption. It would take Jacob twenty years to finally head home and become the bridge builder God had called him to be. Although Jacob had encountered a ladder in Luz, he would still need to wrestle with a snake named Laban to empathize with his brother, Esau. Which takes us to the next step in Jacob's journey toward shedding his snakeskin and finally being the offspring of Eve.

Reflect

Where might God be asking you to be a ladder or bridge builder in your relationships right now? What first step could you take?

_____
_____
_____
_____

When has God met you in an unexpected place or way? How did that encounter change your perspective?

_____
_____
_____
_____

Pray

In prayer, thank God that He shows up in our lives when we don't deserve it.

Day 13

Israel
CHAPTER 11

> Jacob was left alone, and a man wrestled
> with him till daybreak. When the man saw
> that he could not overpower him, he
> touched the socket of Jacob's hip so that
> his hip was wrenched as he wrestled with
> the man. Then the man said, "Let me go,
> for it is daybreak."
>
> But Jacob replied, "I will not let you go
> unless you bless me."
>
> —GENESIS 32:24–26

Think about a time when you were totally shocked—like, biggest-shock-of-your-life kind of thing. A complete "I did not see that coming" curveball.

Do you have it in your mind? Maybe yours was a good moment—more of a surprise than anything else. Well, probably not, since I used the word *shocked* when

I asked you to think of it . . . At any rate, Jacob's shocking moment is not a good one. Long story short, he makes it to his uncle Laban's house and gets to stop sleeping on rocks. He sees one of his uncle's daughters (different time, different place, y'all) and says to himself, *Now, that is the woman for me.* Her name is Rachel. Jacob asks his uncle about the possibility of marrying her, and his uncle makes a counteroffer: "Work for me for seven years, and she's all yours." Jacob is so in love that he agrees.

But on their wedding day, his uncle switches daughters. He sends Leah, who isn't the beauty that Rachel is, down the aisle, heavily veiled (like I said, different time, different place).

In the morning, Jacob realizes what happened. *Boom!*—that level of shock. As in, *Whoa, I did not see that coming.* Really, God knew what He was doing here. If a celestial vision wasn't enough to get Jacob's attention, what would be?

Imagine being Rachel—waiting seven years to marry the man of your dreams but then, the morning of your wedding, being told by your father that there's been a drastic change of plans.

Imagine being Jacob—deceived by a family member who has disguised his older daughter and passed her off as her younger sister. Something about that scenario sounds oddly familiar. Do you remember what it is? What was Jacob's role in that other shocking moment?

Isaac blesses the wrong brother—Jacob instead of Esau.
Jacob marries the wrong sister—Leah instead of Rachel.

Isaac cannot un-bless Jacob and bless Esau.
And Jacob cannot un-marry Leah and marry Rachel.

These stories are intentional parallels. And Laban has replaced Jacob as the new snake. For the first time in his life, Jacob can empathize with his brother, Esau, and finally understand the pain of being deceived by a trusted family member. Jacob, like Esau, has now experienced irreparable and irreversible betrayal, and he can no longer rationalize or justify his snaky, devious behavior toward his brother. When we undergo pain, we finally gain the capacity to be empathetic.

Now Jacob can see Esau with the eyes of a priest instead of a competitor. Because you cannot be a priest without empathy.

How did your own shocking moment change you? Can you see now what God was up to? Was the One who works all things together for good using the shock as an opportunity to get your attention and turn your heart back toward Him?

Jacob has to work another seven years for Rachel. And then his thoughts turn toward home. When Jacob finally decides to stop running away from the call to be a priest and a bridge and heads back home to reconcile with his brother, Genesis 32:1 tells us that "the angels of God met him." This is not Jacob's first time seeing angels on this exact journey, but last time he was a lot younger and walking in the opposite direction.

Twenty years ago, the angels were in a dream.
This time, the angels meet him and interact with him.

Twenty years ago, Jacob was sent to Paddan Aram by his father.
This time, Jacob is sent to Canaan by the Lord, his heavenly Father.

Twenty years ago, he was completely alone.
This time, he sends his entire family ahead so he can be alone again.

Twenty years ago, Jacob changed the name of a town from Luz to Bethel.
This time, Jacob is the one who'll experience a name change.

The climax of this return to Canaan is an epic, all-night wrestling match with a mysterious figure, as we see in today's passage. During the match, "the man . . . touched the socket of Jacob's hip so that his hip was wrenched" (verse 25).

Wrestling is an odd way to interact with someone, yet something about it makes so much sense for Jacob's journey of rehabilitation. Through his whole life, Jacob has gone behind people's backs to deceive them. He's not a confronter at all but rather a passive-aggressive backstabber. Except for this wrestling match. Because there's something oddly forthright and innately honest about wrestling. Wrestling requires face-to-face honesty. It requires intimacy and integrity. The encounter forces Jacob out of his default comfort zone.

At the conclusion of the match, Jacob doesn't win, but he does insist on something: "I will not let you go unless you bless me." Then, God gives him a new name—"Israel," and repeats the promise to give him land and thousands of descendants. And in the next chapters of Genesis, Israel is even reconciled to his brother. That's called being human again. Those are a lot of gains from one wrestling match.

We can be as bold as Jacob: When we're out of our own comfort zones, we can ask for blessings too. It's one of the main ways that God takes our beastliness and returns us to humanity.

Reflect

What shocking moments in your life have led to growth or greater empathy? How has God used those moments?

_____

_____

TAMING THE BEAST   77

_____

_____

How have your struggles with God ultimately led to
blessing? What did those wrestling matches teach you?

_____

_____

_____

_____

Pray

In prayer, welcome the wrestling that is part of relationship with God.

Joseph
CHAPTER 12

> God sent me ahead of you to preserve for
> you a remnant on earth and to save your
> lives by a great deliverance.
> —GENESIS 45:7

After seeing all these family crises and their resolutions, you might wonder to yourself, *Does anybody do this the right way?*

If by "the right way" you mean "without any major hiccups," the answer is decidedly no. Nobody gets through without some pretty serious scrapes. But Genesis ends on a high note. It zooms in on Joseph, one of the twelve sons of Israel—his favorite son, in fact.

Just for a moment, let's pause and look at the way God is working out His promises to this family. Abraham and Sarah couldn't have children for decades—now we're talking about their great-grandchildren. Israel has *twelve* sons. Looks like God is going to make a nation out of them after all! But, of course, not without some bumps in the road.

Are there any "favorite children" in your family lineage? Gosh, I hope not. But sometimes families get into these bad patterns—even families who have seen redemption on the scale of Abraham's descendants. Even if deliberate favoritism isn't part of your current family history, some other strange patterns of dysfunction might be. Yet God wants to redeem you and your family too.

Let's get back to Joseph. He decides to tell his brothers that he had a dream about being greater than all of them. In addition to this, Israel gives him a special coat. The brothers do not respond well to this. They capture Joseph and sell him to slave traders. They dip his special coat in blood and show it to their father, who naturally concludes that his favorite son was eaten by wild animals.

Your original-audience-symbols sensor should be going crazy right now: A fierce animal has devoured Joseph. A wild animal. A beast of the field. A monster of Chaos.

We know that Joseph wasn't actually devoured, so technically their father is incorrect. But we also know that since the Bible speaks in the language of looping symbols and repeating images, Jacob is actually spot on. Joseph has been devoured by fierce and wild animals—his brothers. Which reveals that his brothers are the offspring of the Serpent.

Joseph's brothers are beasts. Monsters. Kings of chaos. Which means that Joseph must be the offspring of Eve and a type of Christ, right?

Let's look at what the text shows us concerning Joseph:

Joseph is sold for some pieces of silver (Genesis 37:28).
He is sold by his brother Judah (verses 26–27). In
Greek, that name is Judas.*
Joseph is tempted by Potiphar's wife yet is without sin
(39:6–9).
Although innocent, he is falsely accused and impris-
oned (verses 19–20).

Sounding familiar yet?

In this story, Joseph's brothers are the animals. The
beasts. The offspring of the Serpent.

Joseph is their prey, but he retains his humanity. Joseph
is the offspring of Eve, and his entire life foreshadows the
ultimate son of the woman—Jesus.

Patterns. Symbols. Images. Loops.

Welcome to reading Eastern literature with Eastern eyes.

Cain is an animal. Ishmael is a wild animal. Esau and
Jacob are both beasts. Joseph's brothers are monsters. All
sons of the Serpent. All crushed by Chaos.

This is the dominant theme and lesson of Genesis: It is
easy for humans to become animals. Our humanity is del-
icate and must be guarded with all the wisdom and
strength we have.

Yet maybe Joseph did learn something from his father's,
grandfather's, and great-grandfather's stories because he
decides, amid all this chaos, to *remain human*. He is taken

* Bible Hub, s.v. "2455. Ioudas," accessed November 29, 2024, https://
biblehub.com/greek/2455.htm.

to Egypt by slave traders and becomes a slave in a prominent house. He shows faithfulness in small things, and he moves up the ladder. There's more to this story, but he's accused of something he didn't do and is thrown into prison. Now, I would be tempted to be bitter at this point. Very bitter. I would be resentfully tossing around the names of each awful brother who got me here in the first place. But Joseph isn't bitter. Eventually, he gets to leave prison after interpreting a dream of Pharaoh's. He again shows faithfulness in small things. And he becomes the second most important person in Pharaoh's palace.

Maybe the real prison isn't incarceration. Maybe it is victimhood and bitterness.

Years later, when Joseph's brothers turn up asking for help, he can help them without any bitterness or anger or resentment getting in the way because he's already forgiven them. The verse for today is part of Joseph's speech to his brothers: "God sent me ahead of you." Not the words I'd use to say, "You pretended I got killed by a wild animal," but I guess Joseph was further along in his "becoming human" process than I may have been. Joseph saw God's hand at work.

This is the secret to preserving our humanity—by retaining our power and authority. The Dragon's agenda is to divide and conquer, so I'm playing right into his hands when I villainize and demonize those who have hurt me. The reason I forgave my father is that I was tired of him having more power over me than I had over myself. I was tired of the Beast using my father to control me.

We're not powerless victims. We're humans made in the image of almighty God, and we're full of power.

Reflect

Where have you seen God's redemptive hand at work in difficult circumstances? How does that give you hope for current challenges?

_____

_____

_____

_____

What small acts of faithfulness could you practice today that might lead to bigger transformation?

_____

_____

_____

_____

Pray

In prayer, ask God for the strength to forgive anyone who has wronged you.

You
CHAPTER 13

> Many live as enemies of the cross of
> Christ. Their destiny is destruction, their
> god is their stomach, and their glory is in
> their shame. Their mind is set on earthly
> things.
>
> —PHILIPPIANS 3:18–19

Over the past week, we've seen that the book of Genesis is studded with incredible characters. God focuses His blessing like a laser beam on one family—the one that will ultimately produce Christ. And if any of us feel like we have crazy families, Jesus can certainly commiserate. Abraham took Isaac up on a mountain, obeying God's command to sacrifice him, only to be stopped by an angel. Then Isaac gave his only blessing to the wrong twin, Jacob. Then Jacob was tricked into marrying the wrong sister and got into a wrestling match with an angel. Jacob's sons sold their own brother Joseph into slavery.

You get what I'm saying. It's a pretty messy family history, which should give us some consolation about our own lives and families. I mean, I'm the son of an addict. I know messy.

Each man from Genesis we've talked about was tempted to be beastly, and sometimes they were. But other times, they stepped up like real humans and worked for reconciliation in their families. No matter what, God continued to work for their redemption. God was always trying to help them be human again and regain what they'd lost to the Dragon in the Garden of Eden so long ago.

Through it all, Scripture is teaching us, in a very subtle and Eastern way, that humans and beasts are not designed to be partners. Adam is designed to rule over them, not partner with them. Adam belongs in the garden. The beasts of the field belong in the wild. God and Adam therefore reject all beasts as suitable partners for humanity. Humans are humans; beasts are beasts. They are categorically different in every way, and Adam has been set apart from the beasts of the field.

> If God primarily speaks through urges,
> through desires,
> through instincts,
> through feelings,
> then all these things begin to function as our gods.

And that is exactly what has happened. Urges, desires, instincts, and feelings have become gods. Since these are now our authorities, we feel we can disobey the commands God actually put into place because the gods that speak to us from the inside hold more weight.

I think this is what Paul is talking about in today's passage when he describes those who oppose Christ, especially when he uses that amazing phrase "their god is their stomach." Have you ever been hangry? You know, angry because you're hungry? When we are so consumed by our urges, desires, and instincts, it's like we get hangry for sin. And when I'm hangry, I know that I'm going to eat.

That's why we must be on our guard. Why we must ask God for His help. Why we must, above all, commit to obeying Him in all things and not our desires. Because our desires can—and will—take over.

Countless believers have sat in my office and told me that they know the Scriptures say not to date non-Christians but they've decided to compromise because they just can't shake some feeling they have. They swear God is talking to them through mystical feelings as opposed to the clarity of His written Word.

The specific issues might get swapped around. But the tug-of-war between what the Bible says and what these believers' personal feelings communicate remains the same.

Forgiveness. Same-sex attraction.
Tithing. Premarital sex.
Church attendance and church engagement.
The list goes on and on.

They know what the Bible says. But there's a feeling or an urge they cannot shake. So, they compromise and obey their instincts, and to avoid feeling guilt and shame, they inevitably begin reinterpreting and then misinterpreting Scripture to align with how "God" spoke to them through their feelings.

What happens when humans *think* they hear God through their urges and instincts? You guessed it— Chaos. What happens when humans hear God through His commands laid out in Scripture? You guessed it— Order.

How have you found yourself resisting God's Order? Are you ever tempted to give more weight to your own feelings than to His words?

Maybe it's not quite as intense as in some of the stories we've looked at, but that resistance to Order is nothing new. We've seen it all in Genesis. Cain resisted God's Order when he took his brother out into the field. Abraham resisted God's Order when he slept with Sarah's maid Hagar. Jacob stole and tricked his way into everything. And today, the temptation to be beasts is just as much a part of our reality as ever.

We live in a world that says we belong to ourselves. It's a world of self-care, self-acceptance, self-love, and self-actualization. Not to mention self-identification and self-awareness and self-expression. We live in a culture that is obsessed with self. This is out of order. It goes against our design. We are lost at sea, in a chaotic storm of selfishness.

No wonder anxiety and loneliness are cultural epidemics. They are simply symptoms of a culture of chaos and expressive individualism.

This is an invitation to dethrone the god of self. To give your life away in service and love to the people of God. This is your opportunity to leave independence and selfishness behind—to reject rampant individualism, to lose your life so you can find it. It's your invitation to be truly human.

Reflect

In what areas of your life do you find yourself trusting feelings over God's words? How might submitting to His Order bring more peace?

_____

_____

_____

_____

Where have you experienced freedom by choosing God's way over self-reliance? What fruit has come from those choices?

_____

_____

_____

_____

Pray

In prayer, ask God to help you set your mind on heavenly things.

WEEK 3

TREADING THE WATERS

What does it look like when a God of Order—an all-good, all-powerful God—interacts with a world given over to Chaos? Why doesn't He just reach down and stop it? Couldn't He do something about all this pain? During this week, I want us to reassess God's character in light of what we now know about Chaos. We're going to consider God's role in the great Flood and the plagues of Egypt—stories in which His character is easy to misinterpret. This week, we'll be considering the mighty waters and the only One who has any say over them.

Flood
CHAPTER 14

> The LORD saw how great the wickedness
> of the human race had become on the
> earth, and that every inclination of the
> thoughts of the human heart was only evil
> all the time. The LORD regretted that he
> had made human beings on the earth, and
> his heart was deeply troubled.
>
> —GENESIS 6:5–6

This week, we're backing up a bit in the chronology. In our first week together, we saw how humanity spiraled into beastliness, destroying the beautiful orderliness of God's creation. In our second week, we watched God restore the humanity to Abraham's family, time and again. Hold on to those two elements—God's Order and God's grace—as we now watch what happens when He interacts with a world of chaos.

We're going to start with a story I'm sure you've heard before: Noah, the ark, and the great Flood. To our modern eyes and ears, the account of the Flood in Genesis 6 can be very confusing. Consider the verses we're looking at today, which come from the perspective of the Almighty Himself. In a certain light, they almost feel like a personal attack. "Only evil all the time"? Really?

Why did an all-good God destroy the world with a giant flood? How can an all-knowing, all-powerful God regret anything? Why doesn't He just change things? Why doesn't He just change *us*?

Let's flip the question around. The Flood account isn't a story of God destroying the earth. Rather, it is a story of how we turned our ordered home into a hell of Chaos, and it took only seven chapters of the biblical story for us to do it. Humans desired a world without God. Of course His heart was deeply troubled—He knew what would happen if He left, but humanity didn't even want Him there. He wouldn't stay without their consent.

The same thing happens now—God doesn't begin His ordering work in our hearts without our invitation. Have you ever wished that God would just fix you? I know I have. I want to skip the growth part. I want to skip the death-to-self part. Just like the people God saw on earth in those earliest days, I get very fixated on my own needs and desires—and one of the things I think I need is for God to act the way I want Him to. The people described in Genesis 6 probably wanted a God they could put in their pockets too. One that never confronted them with the reality of their sin or the necessary pain of change. These people wanted none of that.

When God removed Himself, creation simply reverted to its original state—chaos.

Yahweh wasn't responsible for the fountains of the great *tehom* bursting forth. Leviathan wasn't the culprit who plunged creation back into Chaos. Humans alone had the power to turn our home into our hell. We caused creation to fold in on itself and collapse. Because playing with Chaos eventually leads to drowning in Chaos.

If order invites divine rest, chaos drives God away. And we made it clear—we wanted a world without God, a world of independence and autonomy. We wanted a world ruled by humans as opposed to one ruled by God through humans. We wanted a world free of God's controlling and overbearing rules.

So, God left us alone. Because fortunately, God honors our freewill choices. He'll never force us into His presence. If God didn't honor our free will, He'd be the monster. And if God is a monster, the rest of the Bible ain't worth reading.

Genesis is drilling these ideas into the psyche of its audience because God's character is on the line. If God is a monster, then obeying Him will create just as much chaos. So, Genesis is painting a picture of God that humanity can trust. Because we must trust His character before we can embrace His Order.

Let's turn for a moment and deal with a few personal questions the Flood account brings to the forefront. How would you describe God's character, especially in light of what you've learned about Genesis in the past two weeks?

Is God trustworthy? Why or why not? Has your belief about God's trustworthiness changed over time? What are you still hesitant to give over to Him?

The Flood narrative could easily paint God as a cosmic killjoy and ruthless judge. Yet it is declaring the exact opposite: Humans are on a path of self-destruction, and God recruits a man named Noah to be a partner in saving humans from total extinction by creating a floating temple amid the chaotic waters.

God didn't destroy humans with a flood—the humans had already destroyed themselves. Today's passage tells us that every inclination of their hearts was evil. Can you imagine how that story would have ended had God let things continue? But instead, God came in with a plan of redemption. That's who God is. That's what we see in Scripture over and over. He's not a destroyer; He's a rescuer and a redeemer. Not a petulant child whose plan went wrong—a perfect Father who is willing to try anything to get His children back.

It's impossible to trust God's Order if we can't trust His character. God doesn't drown people; Chaos does. And we have partnered with Chaos to our own detriment and downfall. All God has to do to punish us is simply get up and walk away. That's it. When God leaves, everything is inevitably plunged back into Chaos.

Let's go to the crossroads and find the ancient path so we can grasp what the Flood story is actually trying to teach us.

Reflect

How has your understanding of God's character shifted as you've studied Genesis? What aspects of His nature give you hope?

_____

_____

_____

_____

In what areas of your life do you wish God would just fix things? How might His patient approach actually be better?

_____

_____

_____

_____

Pray

In prayer, ask God to reveal His true character to you.

Day 17

Context
CHAPTER 15

> The LORD said, "My Spirit will not contend
> with humans forever, for they are mortal;
> their days will be a hundred and twenty
> years."
> —GENESIS 6:3

Context is everything when it comes to interpreting ancient texts. Written words can be tricky—they can take on unintentional meanings if we don't have a sense of some crucial aspects: Who wrote this? To whom? Why did they say it? Is it supposed to be a poem, a story, a song, a history? What were they trying to do? Reading Scripture without knowing the context is like making an assumption about a person without enough information. We all know where that leads, and it isn't pretty. Confusion is about the best thing that can happen.

That brings us to today's verse. Most people interpret God's statement here to mean humans can't live beyond 120 years. But I think He is saying something different—

something that relates more to the topic at hand: the coming Flood. I mean, if almost everyone is about to die anyway, why does their potential lifespan matter? I think the God of Order is trying to give a divine warning through the only person who isn't hopelessly lost in chaos—a guy named Noah. What if God is announcing, "My Spirit will not abide with humans forever; their days *with Me* will be 120 more years"? If God is stating that He will not continue living among humans who act sinfully and violently, then everything that follows this announcement makes perfect sense—the cosmos completely collapses because God has no choice but to leave the group chat.

In week 1, we saw that in bringing Order to the Chaos through creation, God had made a temple for Himself. If God is now saying that His Spirit can no longer dwell among humanity, that means His temple is no longer a fit dwelling place—Chaos has overtaken Order, and the human tenants have become squatters in God's palace. Humans have multiplied Chaos to the point that it's unbearable for the divine presence.

The ancient Jewish Qumran community, who diligently copied and wrote commentaries on the Scriptures, also didn't believe that God was limiting lifespans to 120 years. Rather, they believed God was giving Noah 120 years to build a house for His presence because He was scheduling His departure from the land.

So, let's put all the puzzle pieces together. In Genesis 6:3, I think God is saying, "My Spirit will not dwell with humans forever. You have a hundred and twenty years until I will no longer dwell here with you." Is it possible that we've been reading these verses in English incorrectly?

Is the text talking about a God who gave 120 years of warning before the catastrophe or a God who shortened lifespans and then killed everyone? The first interpretation is harmonious with a God of Order—not one who unleashed a flood because He was angry but one who stopped holding back the tide when He had to step away. Darkness isn't a punishment for turning off the lights; it's just what happens when we flip the switch.

As I studied the book of Genesis, my eyes were opened again and again once I understood the proper context of these familiar stories. I couldn't help but wonder, *What else have I misunderstood? What other stories were told to me in a way that would have been so different from the first speakers and the first hearers?*

Context changes everything. This is why chaos ensues when we don't have the right context for Scripture. Because without context, different ideologies can copy the words of the Bible but swap the emphasis and meaning. People—usually those consumed by their desire for power—can distort the words to the point where God isn't a part of the picture anymore.

Maybe you know exactly what I'm talking about all too well. Maybe people who appeared to care about you wielded the words of Scripture in a way that distorted your perception of God's character.

If you've escaped the chaos of fundamentalism but now

you're lost and wandering in the wilderness of an endless and toxic deconstruction journey, I understand your fears. You trusted leaders, and you trusted what they told you. And they betrayed that trust by giving you their *interpretations* of the Bible and telling you those interpretations were authoritative. So now you don't know whom or what to trust. I understand, and I'm inviting you to fall in love with the Scriptures again and encounter them afresh. God's Order doesn't look like the fundamentalism you escaped. Your fears are legitimate, but they don't give you a lifetime pass to run away from God.

No matter what you're afraid of, know this: God wants you to experience His words. He longs to be with you. And Scripture is one of the ways that He offers Himself and His undivided attention to you. It's worth reading again and reading well. It's worth another chance, even if people have hurt you or you're weighed down by all kinds of baggage that seems to feel even heavier when you just look at a Bible.

Friend, it's worth trying again.

Because Genesis is designed to set the record straight and reveal the loving, patient character of God. Genesis is designed for careful meditation. It makes the most sense when placed in context. Sometimes when we read the Bible, there's a gap between what is *said* and what is *meant*. That's not a design flaw; it's a design feature. Because these texts were designed not for casual or careless reading but for faithful and diligent disciples who value what these texts mean as much as what they say.

We're not done with the story of Noah. I mean, we haven't even gotten to the Flood part yet. But I wanted you to have a little different vision of God's character before He steps away and the floodwaters start rising.

Reflect

When have misunderstandings of Scripture affected your view of God? How has proper context helped restore your faith?

_____

_____

_____

_____

What makes it challenging for you to engage with Scripture? How might seeing it through an "Eastern lens" change your approach?

_____

_____

_____

_____

Pray

In prayer, thank God for His goodness.

Temple
CHAPTER 16

> Noah did everything just as God
> commanded him.
>
> —GENESIS 6:22

Other than the part about the animals (which were more than "two by two," as it turns out—if you don't believe me, look at Genesis 7:2–3) and the earth-covering water, what do you remember about the Flood narrative? If the beginning of the story doesn't immediately pop up in your mind, it might be because God gave Noah a bunch of details that were extremely specific and—surprise surprise—significant to the original audience but that are often lost on modern readers.

For a refresher, the first five books of the Bible were put together for the Israelites who had just left Egypt. Some details, patterns, and rhythms are specifically for them. Even the Hebrew word for "ark" was copped from the Egyptian word *tevah*. The original audience of Genesis are freed slaves steeped in Egyptian culture—they are familiar with the Egyptian version of the *tevah* and have seen these idol-filled shrines floating down the Nile. And the part of Genesis 6 that we glaze over, all the strange instructions with odd measurements, would have grabbed their attention. Maybe it's just because I haven't been in the right places, but I've never heard a children's song about Noah and the Flood with the word *cubit* in it. Yet God's instructions to Noah would sound familiar to the Israelites, echoing the directives He had given them for building a sanctuary for His presence.

God brings order to chaos by creating temple spaces. Out of the chaos of creation, God planted a temple garden. And out of the chaos of the Flood, God had Noah construct a floating temple that sustained human life amid the chaotic floodwaters. However, the Bible doesn't *tell* us that Noah's ark was a temple. It *shows* us. The instructions for building the ark tell us what we need to know—as long as we're looking for it.

Take the word *tevah*. Why would God have Noah build a boat with the same name as an Egyptian dwelling place for gods and idols? Maybe God wants to fill His *tevah* with creatures made in His image. Maybe this is more than a boat. Maybe Noah is constructing a temple that will be carried on the raging waters of the Flood. In other words, perhaps the ark is a dwelling place for God. It could be that the world needed ordered sacred space so we could dwell with God again.

Maybe you feel like God is offering you a temple when

your circumstances suggest you need a boat. Maybe you need to restore order to your chaotic life and don't see how a temple is relevant to your problems. Allow me to help. God's Order precedes His presence, and His presence always leads us into more order.

Let's look at the words of Psalm 46:1–3:

> God is our refuge and strength,
>   an ever-present help in trouble.
> Therefore we will not fear, though the earth give way
>   and the mountains fall into the heart of the sea,
> though its waters roar and foam
>   and the mountains quake with their surging.

I think the writer of this psalm was reflecting on the Flood story when he penned these words. Noah built a dwelling place for the divine presence; it just so happens that the temple he built was a boat. Genesis emphasized this vessel as a temple, but that's visible only with Eastern eyes.

This temple, built exactly to God's specifications, outlasted the Flood. It rose above the churning and roiling waters of chaos and made it to dry land. Noah chose to be in God's presence, and he made it to the other side of the catastrophe.

I have a hunch that if we were to diligently present ourselves as temples of the divine presence, God would take up residence within us and His wisdom would begin to bring order to our chaos. And together, we could bring order to the cosmos, and the earth would be full of the glory of God again.

Is it possible for Christians to live in such a way that we attract and hasten the return of Christ? I don't know. But I've decided to live as though it is. Some—okay, most—of these ways of life aren't big, showy expressions of goodness. They're small. I'm talking about having patience with my upset child. Sharing coffee with my neighbor. Speaking about my marriage with hope, in all the conversations I find myself in. Listening to others—actually listening— and giving them whatever space they need. Doing the thousand little things that come with my job with prayer and peace instead of resentment and wishing I were somewhere else. Opening my hands and giving to others out of the abundant resources God has given me.

Because I want to be like Noah—I want to do everything just as God commanded me. I want to help usher in His temple presence that way. I know that God wants to be here, on earth, with us despite our inclinations toward chaos. And I'm going to let Him in. I'm going to stay with Him.

I've decided to contend for order, conquer the chaos, build a temple, offer myself as a living sacrifice, and pray for the return of the King. I won't do it perfectly. But I want you to join me anyway—just as I want to join in the things you're already doing for the kingdom.

Reflect

What small things could you do today to help build a dwelling place for God's presence? How might these actions bring order to chaos?

_____

_____

_____

_____

Where in your life do you feel God offering you a temple when you think you need a boat? What might He be teaching you through this?

_____

_____

_____

_____

Pray

In prayer, thank God that He remains present with us always.

Active Grace
CHAPTER 17

> God said, "This is the sign of the covenant
> I am making between me and you and
> every living creature with you, a covenant
> for all generations to come: I have set my
> rainbow in the clouds, and it will be the
> sign of the covenant between me and the
> earth."
>
> **—GENESIS 9:12–13**

We're coming to the end of the Flood narrative, the original "fresh start" story. Spoiler alert: The boat eventually landed. The temple that God dwelled in with Noah floated over the chaos for months. It rained for forty days and forty nights, and then the occupants of the floating temple waited for the waters of chaos to recede. Once again, God separated land from water. And there was a new beginning.

Has your perception of God's character shifted as you've

reconsidered the Flood story? Is He a God of wrath or a God of grace? Or is it possible that His character encompasses both? It's hard for us, finite beings that we are, to handle paradox—two incompatible qualities existing simultaneously. But this is exactly what Genesis invites us into. It's hard to reconcile "fresh start" with "wrath of God." But we're going to make the attempt today as we consider the conclusion of the Flood account.

I think we should ask whether the interpretation of the Flood I'm presenting fits with the picture the rest of Scripture paints concerning God's character. Already in the Bible, we've seen God punish Adam, Eve, and Cain, so there's a track record to check.

Once Adam and Eve ate from the tree, did God kill them? No—no, He didn't.

Zero acts of immediate capital punishment.
Zero executions performed at the crime scene.
Zero heads rolled.

What did God do instead? He removed them from His presence and revoked their access to the tree of life. Active wrath would have required their immediate deaths, based on the consequences God clearly outlined. Yet He simply removed them from the garden, and since they couldn't eat from the tree of life, they were forced to confront the reality of their eventual expiration. Was this a simple reset, an aspect of God's wrath, or both?

Think about a fresh start you've experienced in your own life—a time when you had to start over, perhaps from scratch. (Maybe the description *fresh* is a little too chipper for what happened to you.) During that time, what was your opinion about God? Did you feel that He was giving you grace to start again or punishing you for something?

It's easy to think of God's wrath as active and His grace as passive. Many of us are consumed by anxiety to the point that we always think the other shoe is about to drop, and we transpose this feeling onto God's character: *He's up there waiting to catch me doing something wrong.* That's a belief in active wrath. Many of us also think He gives grace only when we work for it. I know, I know—grace alone. That's what we all say we believe. But I want you to consider your heart: Do you believe you need to earn God's love? That's a belief in passive grace.

Some of our first instincts about this can lead us in the wrong direction. Maybe we've seen active wrath and passive grace from people in authority, and we sometimes expect God to act like a much bigger, much more powerful person. But His character has far more depth and mystery than ours do. We need to look at God's Word instead of our experiences and expectations. What we find in Scripture is a God who acts in *active* grace and *passive* wrath.

In the garden, Adam and Eve encountered God's passive wrath as opposed to His active wrath. God chose grace instead of judgment. There's a monumental difference between actively killing them and simply removing them from a source of life they were never entitled to in the first place.

God's very first act of judgment provides a pattern. God opts for passive wrath over active wrath. He blends a healthy amount of mercy with His justice.

When God departs from His creation or removes Himself from our lives, everything inevitably folds in on itself and sinks back into Chaos. That's how the passive wrath of God works. But we must acknowledge the flip side of the coin—active grace.

In the NRSV wording of today's passage, God says, "I have set my bow in the clouds." The Hebrew word used here simply means "bow."* And the image Yahweh is meaning to evoke is of an archer's bow.

Here's a moment where the NIV translators meant well by making the text easier to understand, but good intentions can sometimes remove the set of images that the original audience would have had in their minds.

An archer's bow is a weapon, and Yahweh is using this image to communicate something important concerning His character and His covenant. If you imagine a rainbow as an archer's weapon in the clouds, one thing becomes very clear—the arrow is pointing away from the earth and toward the heavens.

---

* *Enhanced Brown-Driver-Briggs Hebrew and English Lexicon,* ed. Francis Brown, Samuel Rolles Driver, and Charles Augustus Briggs (Oak Harbor, Wash.: Logos Library System, 2000), s.v. "*qeset.*"

Yahweh is saying to Noah and to all humanity, "Next time I flood the earth with water, it will be because the arrow pierced Me, not y'all." The proof that humanity and Yahweh are in covenant is the fact that He's willing to be on the receiving end of the archer's arrow rather than make us pay the penalty of our sin. His covenant with Noah is essentially Yahweh saying, "This is going to hurt Me more than it's going to hurt you"—and actually meaning it.

You can't find grace more active than that. This is the character of our God. May He give us the grace to trust in what He has revealed.

Reflect

When have you experienced God's active grace in your life? How did it change your perspective of Him?

_____

_____

_____

_____

How does seeing God's wrath as passive and His grace as active reshape your view of difficult circumstances?

_____

_____

_____

_____

Pray

In prayer, thank God that His grace is active and not passive. Ask for the grace to trust what He has revealed.

Moses

CHAPTER 18

> Moses and Aaron went to Pharaoh and did just as the LORD commanded. Aaron threw his staff down in front of Pharaoh and his officials, and it became a snake.
>
> —EXODUS 7:10

My whole life, I believed that Beren*stein* Bears was the correct spelling for the book series I read and enjoyed as a kid. You can probably imagine my confusion and utter shock when I found out that's never been the spelling. According to every single internet search that anyone can find—and the official website*—it's always been Beren*stain* Bears.

I'm ashamed to admit that my initial reaction was to assume there was some kind of conspiracy theory. Some-

---

* "The History of Berenstain Bears," The Berenstain Bears, accessed December 2, 2024, https://berenstainbears.com/about/.

one must have gotten rid of all the copies with the original spelling from my childhood and replaced them with this new weird one. I'm not alone, by the way. Millions of people incorrectly remember the spelling of this book series. I know because we've all found each other on the internet.

There's a term for this phenomenon—where a significant portion of the population incorrectly remembers an event or shares a memory of an event that did not actually occur. It's called the Mandela effect.

Did the Fruit of the Loom logo ever have a cornucopia with fruit pouring out?
Does Pikachu's tail have a black tip?
Does Mr. Monopoly wear a monocle?

If you said yes to any of those, you're probably under the influence of the Mandela effect.* Because the correct answer to all those questions is no.

All of these are communal false memories and popular examples of the Mandela effect. However, this phenomenon extends beyond pop culture. For myriad reasons, many Christians have communal false memories of biblical stories and events. Like Moses throwing down his staff before Pharaoh and it becoming a snake. That's our verse

---

* Jacopo Prisco, "The 'Mandela Effect' Describes the False Memories Many of Us Share. But Why Can't Scientists Explain It?," CNN World, September 18, 2023, www.cnn.com/2023/09/18/world/mandela-effect-collective-false-memory-scn/index.html.

for today, and it's the translation most of us grew up with. But it contributes to a communal false memory. So, what actually happened?

Let's insert the Hebrew word used in the last part of today's verse: "Aaron threw his staff down in front of Pharaoh and his officials, and it became a [*tannin*]."

I hope you remember that word from earlier in our study.

A *tannin*. A dragon.
A Chaos dragon.
A sea monster.

Talk about a plot twist.

That's a bit different than picturing a couple of snakes from the zoo's reptile exhibit slithering on the floor of Pharaoh's throne room in front of Moses, his brother, and some other guys in robes. An actual monster appears— that's terrifying. More than that, the appearance of a *tannin* in the middle of Moses's story in Exodus reveals that this is profoundly connected to what we've already read in Genesis.

But the dragon that roars to life when Aaron throws down his staff is not the only dragon in the throne room that day. Pharaoh is a monster too. *The Prince of Egypt* movie really messed that up for most of us, painting Pharaoh as sympathetic and everything, but Scripture brings a different perspective. You have to remember, this is the guy who ordered that all the Israelite baby boys be thrown into the river. He's not just a ruler—he's a dragon. And since a decent portion of the original audience had lived through these events, this perspective would have been obvious to them.

These comparisons continue throughout Scripture. Rahab was a famous Chaos dragon known by name throughout the ancient world,* but here Isaiah uses this name as a substitute for Pharaoh. Isaiah sees Pharaoh through the lens of an ancient worldview, and now we can as well.

The biblical authors see Pharaoh as a dragon. Moses. Ezekiel. Isaiah. They all view Pharaoh this way.

So, what does Yahweh equip Moses with as he goes to confront the most powerful human leader on the planet? You guessed it. A staff that can turn into a dragon.

I want to check in on how you're feeling right now. It's brain bending to discover a Mandela effect in your understanding of Scripture. Sometimes, discoveries like this can send us reeling in the wrong direction: *Why did no one ever tell me this? Were they—my church leaders, my family members, the people who taught me about Jesus—keeping things from me?*

I think, in most cases, the answer to that is no. These communal misunderstandings are typically just that— communal. Beyond the cultural barriers to interpreting Scripture, it's often just hard to truly understand what

---

* Klaas Spronk, "Rahab," in *Dictionary of Demons and Deities in the Bible,* ed. Karel van der Toorn, Bob Becking, and Pieter W. van der Horst, 2nd ed. (Grand Rapids, Mich.: Wm. B. Eerdmans, 1999), 684–86.

God is communicating to us. Think of the Israelites, who disobeyed God and worshipped idols. Think of the disciples, who interacted with Jesus *in person* and still had a rough time understanding what He was saying to them. Is it any wonder that we have trouble grasping what God is saying to us too? Offer grace to yourself. Offer grace to others. And marvel at the mysteries Scripture contains.

It's not a rainbow; it's a *bow,* pointed at the heart of heaven. It's not a snake; it's a *dragon.* Just how deep is this rabbit hole, exactly? In the beauties of His Word and the depth of His stories, God draws you closer to Him, turning your heart toward His. Since He's the same God we saw ordering creation in Genesis, we know that He's willing to take His time to do the job right.

I want you to integrate these new discoveries about Scripture without a hint of resentment. I want you to think, *Wow, there's so much more to discover in God's Word.*

Reflect

How does your approach to Scripture change when you view biblical examples of the Mandela effect as invitations to dig deeper? What questions intrigue you?

_____

_____

_____

_____

When have mysteries in your faith led to deeper understanding rather than doubt? What did that teach you
about God?

_____

_____

_____

_____

Pray

In prayer, thank God that you have a whole lifetime to
learn about what His Word is saying to you.

Pharaoh
CHAPTER 19

> Moses returned to the LORD and said,
> "Why, Lord, why have you brought trouble
> on this people? Is this why you sent me?
> Ever since I went to Pharaoh to speak in
> your name, he has brought trouble on this
> people, and you have not rescued your
> people at all."
>
> —EXODUS 5:22–23

Moses and the Israelites weren't freed immediately. It reminds me of how creation wasn't just "there" instantly. God worked—pulling apart, bringing together, untangling hopeless knots. But Moses had some choice words for the Almighty: "You have not rescued your people at all."

Just to continue my active-grace, passive-wrath distinction from a few days ago, I don't think a God who was bent on active wrath would have tolerated that statement from

Moses. So, what does our God do? He reassures Moses. At the beginning of Exodus 6, He basically says, "I will take care of this. I will take care of you. I've heard you, and I'm doing something about it." Just like a patient, powerful father—which, after all, He is.

How will God work this out? Well, He knows that the people have heard the stories of Abraham, Isaac, and Jacob—their great-great-great-and-so-on-grandfathers. So He uses patterns that are similar to those we've already seen. You see, these people understood that history repeats itself, and the story of their liberation leans into that.

The author of Exodus intentionally portrays Moses and Pharaoh in juxtaposition to each other. Pharaoh is the seed of the Serpent, and Moses is clearly the seed of the woman. Whereas Pharaoh is a king of Chaos, Moses will bring Order to Israel. Pharaoh drowns babies in the Nile, but Moses survives the Nile as a baby. Pharaoh enslaves; Moses liberates.

It could easily seem as though Yahweh is being unjust, extreme, and unreasonably cruel as the plagues pull Egypt back into Chaos. But we must unearth the context beneath the surface before we jump to conclusions. The Flood narrative has already established that Yahweh is loving, gracious, kind, and merciful, and this account of the plagues cannot erase or undermine that.

So, we must ask an important question: Who was Pharaoh according to the Egyptian religious pantheon?

Pharaoh proclaimed himself to be the incarnation of

the Egyptian god Horus, and he was believed to be the son of Ra, the sun god. He represented the entire pantheon of gods to the Egyptian people. Simply put, Pharaoh was a god.

This detail changes everything. Because Yahweh is going to engage with this self-proclaimed god as if he's actually a god. And by the end of the narrative, Pharaoh will know that he is neither the incarnation of Horus nor the son of Ra but a mere mortal whose arrogance has provoked the wrath of the one true God.

Of course, it takes him more than a minute to start believing this. After all, Pharaoh has been told since childhood that he, as the leader of the Egyptian people, is a god. I know that might sound ridiculous. But how long does it take us to finally believe we're not actually in control of our lives? How many chaotic situations do we have to live through? How long must we grasp for control? I wish I could say that I relented to total trust in God the moment I realized I wasn't in charge of my life, but I hung on for a while. And I still have relapses.

Sometimes we just don't let go. And then, what happens next isn't a punishment; it's passive wrath. We can't do anything on our own. We can't hold anything together. When we try—perhaps especially when we try as hard as we can—things start to fall apart to the tune of ten great plagues in Egypt. Chaos *everywhere*.

But Pharaoh doesn't know this at the beginning of the story. He actually believes that he's got this and that the

Israelites are not God's chosen people but his rightful property. That's his starting point. And it's why the challenge from Moses doesn't faze him one bit.

Since a deity should be able to keep their creation from falling into chaos, Yahweh will prove to Pharaoh that he is a mere human by sending plagues of de-creation and Chaos on the land of Egypt. Yahweh's response to Pharaoh is layered, brilliant, and designed to demonstrate that Pharaoh is utterly dependent on the only God who can pull creation out of Chaos and sustain Order.

Remember, creation is the process whereby Yahweh brought Order out of Chaos. The plagues are simply a reversal of that process. In other words, the plagues occur when God isn't holding back the Chaos anymore. They fall firmly in the category of passive wrath.

As the people of Israel leave Egypt, God is aware that they desperately need Order to be restored to their lives. They've lived as slaves in a culture of immorality, injustice, and idolatry for centuries. So, once they've passed through the Red Sea and experienced the salvation and deliverance of Yahweh, it's time for Moses to give them the Law.

God brings liberty to His people by removing their physical chains of bondage and oppression, and He continues the work of liberation by bringing Order into their lives through the law of Moses. Remember, they had been slaves for generations. They had been told what to do all their lives. They had been told that they were less than, that they deserved to be slaves, that this was all they were good for. And maybe they believed it. So, this new, very comprehensive set of laws their God was giving them would help them unwind all of that. Each law told them that they were precious, beloved, and, more than anything, God's own people.

Yahweh always liberates His people not only from the sin of slavery but also from the slavery of sin—both then and now.

Reflect

What areas of control are you struggling to release to God? What makes this surrender difficult?

_____

_____

_____

_____

When has God's patient work in your life produced better results than a quick fix would have? What did you learn through the process?

_____

_____

_____

_____

Pray

In prayer, ask God for the patience to wait for His promises.

Day 22

Tabernacle
CHAPTER 20

> Have them make a sanctuary for me, and I
> will dwell among them. Make this
> tabernacle and all its furnishings exactly
> like the pattern I will show you.
> —EXODUS 25:8–9

Where were we in our story? Pharaoh is tested, and everyone in Egypt sees that he's just a man. He can't handle the weight of the world. He can't hold back the plagues. There is a God of Order—but Pharaoh isn't He. After losing his own firstborn son in the final plague, Pharaoh lets the Israelites go. Of course, he then has a change of heart and chases after them, only to be drowned in the Red Sea with his army.

After all this, the Israelites have no doubts about their one true God, right? I mean—after seeing the darkness, the locusts, the river of blood? Experiencing Him separate the sea so they could walk on dry land? Well, not quite. The Israelites struggle tremendously.

For a moment, let me say something about faith journeys that have some ups and downs—journeys of believers who wander and falter and fail. Have you ever counted how many times in Exodus the Israelites wish that they could return to Egypt? It's a lot. They get the deliverance they've been asking God for, for generations. And then they wish that they could go back and eat cucumbers again. I'm being serious. So, if you've ever felt the thrill of following God and then, the next day, found yourself totally resistant to His grace and order in your life, you aren't alone.

Up-and-down people—like me and maybe like you—need order. And we need God to impose it on us because we can't do it for ourselves.

Reading today's verse might remind you of Noah, of God asking someone to follow His exact directives. God won't coexist with chaos. He gets rid of it. Once God leads His people through the chaos of the Red Sea, it's time to bring order to their lives. It's time to take them back to the garden—an ordered and sanctified space where God can dwell among them. So, God instructs them to build a tent for His presence—a tabernacle designed to restore cohabitation between God and humanity.

When you get to Exodus 25 and start reading the instructions for this tent, it's easy to get bogged down by the details. Outer coverings of ram and goatskins. Linen curtains woven with blue, purple, and red designs. A floor-mounted golden candelabra with seven lamps. A large bronze altar made from an acacia wood frame with horns on the corners.

Actually, there are so many details that it should lead the curious reader to wonder whether more is going on here than the mere construction of a tent. Not to mention, there's no Home Depot or Hobby Lobby, so where are they getting all these construction materials and arts and crafts supplies?

To answer that question, we need to look back at the time right after the final plague, the one that really put Pharaoh in his place. Before heading to the Red Sea, "the Israelites did as Moses instructed and asked the Egyptians for articles of silver and gold and for clothing. The LORD had made the Egyptians favorably disposed toward the people, and they gave them what they asked for; so they plundered the Egyptians" (Exodus 12:35–36).

They walked away from Egypt with materials for their own tabernacle, receiving these rich items as gifts from the people who once enslaved them. That's incredible! Think about it—the Israelites will adorn their tabernacle, where God will dwell with them, with these symbols of their deliverance. What once held them captive will now hang in their temple. This is redemption—this is God restoring order, making everything new.

God speaks seven times in Exodus* to give Moses the instructions for the tabernacle. Can you think of another

---

* The seven sections of tabernacle instructions in Exodus are found here: (a) 25:1–30:10; (b) 30:11–16; (c) 30:17–21; (d) 30:22–33; (e) 30:34–38; (f) 31:1–11; and (g) 31:12–17.

time when the construction of something was split into a seven-part process? Yeah, the creation account in Genesis. And the seventh time God gives directions for the tabernacle, it's all about keeping the Sabbath. Clearly, there's a "connection between the building of the tabernacle and the seven days of creation, both of which involve six creative acts culminating in a seventh-day rest."*

As long as the people of God carve out ordered space for the divine presence, it's as if the effects of the Fall are neutralized. God has offered His people a road to experience restored Order.

The construction of the tabernacle isn't about building. It's about new creation, and the same Creator who pulled this world out of Chaos is at work again with a new fledgling nation of freed slaves. The construction of the tabernacle is about Order ruling over Chaos—Sabbath rest and reentry into Eden and God providing refuge for His people amid chaotic waters and ravenous wilderness.

God does the same thing with us now. He's calling us back into His Order, to His temple rest. Whether it's the chaos of sin or of slavery, He's ready to draw you out. He wants to reorder your life. You can yield the burden of control back to the only One who has any in the first place, and you can find your place in wholehearted worship.

---

* Peter Enns, *Exodus,* The NIV Application Commentary (Grand Rapids, Mich.: Zondervan, 2000), 509.

Welcome to the world of Scripture. Where Noah's ark is really about the tabernacle. But then you find out that the tabernacle is really about creation. Which means Noah's ark is about creation too because each loop gives new meaning to the last loops—and there are more loops here than on a roller coaster at Six Flags.

Welcome to the mystery.

Welcome to the lifelong pursuit of wisdom.

Welcome to an Eastern way of engaging with the text.

Reflect

How have you seen God weave unlikely elements into your redemption story? What does this reveal about His character?

_____

_____

_____

_____

What materials in your life (experiences, relationships, resources) might God want to use to build His dwelling place in you?

_____

_____

_____

_____

Pray

In prayer, thank God that He can weave anything into your redemption.

WEEK 4

READING THE GOSPELS

If you're wondering what Jesus has to do with any of this, let me assure you—He is the piece that links everything together. We needed the past three weeks to lay the groundwork of what we're going to discover about Jesus, the Prince of Peace, the one who fulfills everything that was written in Genesis. So now that we've considered Genesis with a more Eastern perspective, maybe we'll be surprised by Jesus in the ways His first followers were. How does Jesus interact with chaos? What happens when He, in the flesh, meets again with the *tannin* and the *tehom*? The answers to those questions lead us deeper in our understanding of who Jesus of Nazareth really is.

Pattern

CHAPTER 21

> As soon as Jesus was baptized, he went
> up out of the water. At that moment
> heaven was opened, and he saw the Spirit
> of God descending like a dove and
> alighting on him. And a voice from heaven
> said, "This is my Son, whom I love; with
> him I am well pleased."
>
> —MATTHEW 3:16–17

I don't think you'll be too surprised at this point that we need to go back to the beginning of Genesis for a recap—so much is contained in those first verses. There's a reason we start there, and there's a reason we must return there to grow in our understanding of God's plan. I also want you to pay attention to a pattern we find in those very first lines of the Bible. Here's Genesis 1:2:

Now the earth was formless and empty, darkness
was over the surface of the deep, and the Spirit of
God was hovering over the waters.

Chaos. Water. Wind.

Tohu va-vohu. Tehom. Ruach. In that specific order.
We're two verses into the biblical text, and we're already
halfway into a pattern that will persist and permeate
through the entire narrative of the Bible.

In the next verse, God speaks, and the authority of His
spoken word moves creation from Chaos to Order. For the
next several days of creation, God will impose His divine
Order on creation as the Chaos bows and submits to the
will and wisdom of the Creator.

Order never happens by accident or chance. Order requires intentionality.

So far, then, we have Chaos, water, wind, word, and
Order. We're five steps into our six-step pattern, and the
pattern will always end with a test.

Because boundaries aren't boundaries until they're
tested. God will test Adam and Eve to see whether they
will partner with Him to extend the boundaries of divine
Order or choose to partner with the Dragon and become
agents of Chaos.

Spoiler alert: They fail the test, and creation is plunged
back into Chaos. Five steps forward. Six steps back. And
the cycle starts over.

This six-step pattern will appear over and over again:

Chaos.
Deep waters.
Wind or Spirit of God.
The voice of Yahweh.
Divine Order.
A failed test.
Repeat.

The same template shows up all throughout the Old Testament, and the Jewish people would have known to listen for it. The Flood account in Genesis. The Exodus out of Egypt. Decades later, the Israelites claiming the land of Canaan for their own. You can dive into each of these examples in your own Bible, but you'll see the same thing repeated—the six-part Chaos cycle, always ending with a failed test.

Let's turn our attention to Matthew 3:13–17, which includes today's verses. Do you see pieces of the Chaos cycle? Put yourselves in the shoes of Matthew's original audience. When He's baptized, Jesus comes *up out of the waters.* Next, the *Spirit of God* is there. And then, the *voice of God,* coming down from the heavens . . . *"This is my Son, whom I love; with him I am well pleased."* Woah. That should be familiar. We're in the middle of something, and it's the chaos cycle. Would you be surprised if I told you that the next chapter of Matthew begins with Jesus's temptation in the wilderness? He's headed toward a test. But the original audience would have known to anticipate something like that.

Imagine what they think as they hear and read that Jesus goes into the deep waters of the Jordan to be baptized by John. That the Spirit of almighty God descends on Jesus in the form of a dove, hovering above the deep waters. That a voice from heaven begins to speak as Jesus is in the Chaos waters, with the Spirit brooding over the deep. Imagine their thoughts when they learn that Jesus is getting baptized not to be cleansed of sin but to do what is proper—to establish Order and to fulfill all righteousness.[*]

Imagine them listening with bated breath as Jesus is immediately led out into the wilderness to be tested. This is where things always go wrong. This is the point where we always take six steps back after five solid steps forward.

The Chaos cycle isn't just biblical; it's a personal reality for each of us. Everyone's personal chaos cycle will look different, but I submit that it still follows the pattern.

What resolutions do you find yourself making? After experiencing God's grace and coming to a new understanding, maybe you resolve to become more responsible in some way. You tell yourself, *I'll get it right this time—I'm going to be kind to my family members. I'll do what I need to do when I need to do it. No more procrastinating. No more excessive consumption.*

We make resolutions like this all the time, hoping to

---

[*] *A Greek-English Lexicon of the New Testament,* trans. Joseph Henry Thayer (New York: Harper & Brothers, 1889), s.v. "*kētos.*"

finally escape our personal cycles of chaos. Then, those moments of testing come, and we descend right back into the swirl. We're found wanting. We're stuck in the chaos cycle, unable to redeem ourselves. We cannot break the Chaos cycle on our own—we need a redeemer. One to stand in for us.

As we turn to other moments in Jesus's life and ministry, let us remember that His entire ministry started by standing in the floodwaters of the Jordan as an agent of God's Order and a Prince of Peace. Everything Jesus does afterward is colored by the inaugural moment of His baptism and His subsequent wilderness testing. Jesus is the Chaos Crusher. Jesus is the Beast-taming, Dragon-conquering, Chaos-crushing Messiah. Born as the offspring of the woman to crush the head of the Dragon. Born to break the cycle of Chaos so that all God's children may be free.

Reflect

What personal chaos cycles do you recognize in your life? How might understanding these patterns help you break them?

_____

_____

_____

_____

Where have you seen God's consistent work to bring order in your life? What hope does this give you?

_____

_____

_____

_____

Pray

In prayer, thank God that He keeps speaking into your life.

Temptation

CHAPTER 22

> Again, the devil took him to a very high
> mountain and showed him all the
> kingdoms of the world and their splendor.
> "All this I will give you," he said, "if you
> will bow down and worship me."
>
> Jesus said to him, "Away from me, Satan!
> For it is written: 'Worship the Lord your
> God, and serve him only.'"
>
> Then the devil left him, and angels came
> and attended him.
>
> —MATTHEW 4:8–11

Yesterday, we left Jesus right at that sixth step in the Chaos cycle: Chaos, waters, Spirit of God, voice of God, Order, and then . . . The first people who read Matthew's gospel were steeped in the Jewish tradition and would have known that a test was coming. Jesus is about to step into the ring with the *tannin,* and the audience knows it. Sure enough, Jesus goes through the Chaos waters of baptism and is immediately cast out into the wilderness. Why? So He could subdue the Chaos on our behalf and we could all regain access to the garden.

The story of Jesus's temptation tells us something powerful about prayer and Scripture. After He's baptized, Jesus leaves behind His friends and family to fast and pray in the desert for forty days. Lest we think of this as some kind of self-care stint, let's remember that He was tempted three times by the devil. He wasn't hiding from this kind of temptation—He went out to face it directly. And when we pray, we're doing the same thing. We're not hiding from our problems or our responsibilities; we're confronting the spiritual realities of our lives.

Jesus is driven out into the realm of Chaos for the confrontation with the Dragon that we've been anticipating since Genesis 3:15. The Spirit compels Jesus to confront the Dragon on the Dragon's *own turf.*

Jesus is not on the defensive.

Jesus seeks to confront Chaos head-on.

Jesus is going in to fight. And the Dragon doesn't have to be told twice—he shows up with all his favorite temptations when Jesus is at His weakest and most vulnerable. Food. Power. Wealth.

And Jesus deflects every single one with God's Word.

The Dragon's words are well chosen, but Jesus's responses are even better. Why? Because at this critical moment, He uses scripture to back up His actions. It's apparent that He has spent much time with His Father in prayer and committed His Father's words to heart—to the point that when the big test comes, He is ready. He doesn't fail; He passes. Because the practice of prayer and scripture was a consistent part of His life.

Stepping out of the chaos cycle starts with committing to those steps of praying and learning Scripture, as tiny as they may seem. Of course, we need Christ's strength to do it. We could never do this on our own. Many of us have attempted to tame lions but have never tamed our lusts. We've attempted to calm storms but have never calmed our souls. We desire control over others, but we lack the best kind of control—self-control. And whenever we become obsessed with controlling externals as opposed to internal matters, we create chaos. So much of our anxiety is rooted in our desire to control things that aren't and will never be in our control.

Knowing all this about us, Jesus goes out into the wilderness to confront the Dragon. He goes off into the desert to tame the beasts, to crush the Chaos, and to plunder the Dragon and rob him of his ill-gotten gains.

He who knew no sin was treated as sin so that we might become the righteousness of God (2 Corinthians 5:21). This is the scandalous exchange and great reversal of the gospel: He who was perfect was treated as a sinner so that sinners could be treated as perfect.

Adam and Eve are expelled out of the garden.
Jesus is expelled into the wilderness.

Adam and Eve eat the fruit in the garden.
So, Jesus fasts in the wilderness.

Adam and Eve fail to subdue the animal within the
garden.
So, Jesus has to subdue the animal within and without
in the wilderness.

Jesus was driven out so that we could be brought back in. The wilderness is not our fate. We're not stuck out in the desert. We can return to the garden—we can enter and find rest for our souls.

Immediately following the binding of the Dragon in the desert, Jesus begins preaching the good news. The Cross has not yet happened, but the gospel announcement of freedom and deliverance can go out like a clarion call because the defeat of the Dragon has begun. Satan has been bound, and now Jesus will begin setting captives free and thereby plundering the Dragon.

Jesus knows what temptations feel like because He's felt the pull of them Himself. And He knows how to deflect these temptations: with the truth about God and about the coming kingdom. Jesus is ready and waiting to show us what life looks like outside the cycle of Chaos.

Reflect

When have small acts of faithfulness prepared you for bigger challenges? What practices help strengthen your faith?

_____

_____

_____

_____

How does seeing Jesus face temptation change your approach to your own struggles? What encouragement do you find in His example?

_____

_____

_____

_____

Pray

In prayer, ask God for the strength to be consistent in the small things.

Tempest
CHAPTER 23

> One day Jesus said to his disciples, "Let us go over to the other side of the lake." So they got into a boat and set out. As they sailed, he fell asleep. A squall came down on the lake, so that the boat was being swamped, and they were in great danger.
>
> —LUKE 8:22–23

Have you ever been afraid for your safety because of something the weather was doing? Think of the wildest weather event you've ever experienced. Maybe it was a tornado, hurricane, flood, or fire—or just a really bad thunderstorm. I don't judge. I'm not very outdoorsy, so it all feels pretty wild to me. I'm serious—even the sunshine is kind of a stretch for me sometimes. Anyway, go back to the moment where you were in the middle of crazy weather that was totally out of your control. Something way, way bigger than you was going on. What did you feel, think, and do? Did you freeze or freak out—or some combination of both?

Luke's account of Jesus and the disciples crossing the Sea of Galilee is one of the most retold stories from his gospel. Since we've heard it so often, sometimes we don't connect to the raw fear the disciples were feeling. We're reading about what happened, but they lived it. That's why I want you to think about the sheer power of the weather and the way you've experienced it in your own life.

Let me point out one more detail to set up this story. The account of Jesus's temptation is recorded in Matthew, Mark, and Luke. Luke's version is almost identical to what we have in Matthew—except for one small addition at the end of the story. Luke 4:13 tells us, "When the devil had finished all this tempting, he left him until an opportune time."

Wait a minute. An opportune time? Am I missing something? I assumed that Jesus's passing these three tests would put an end to the struggle between Him and the Dragon forever. I assumed this was a decisive victory. However, the Bible teaches us one of the most valuable lessons concerning Chaos and its cycle with this detail found in Luke's gospel.

All right, here's the story of what I believe was the Dragon's "opportune time." Jesus tells His disciples that it's time to get in the boat. He's had a full day of ministry, so He falls asleep. Then a giant storm kicks up. The thunder is booming, the lightning is flashing on every side, and water is pouring into the boat—which, by the way, was not big. The disciples wake Jesus up, exclaiming, "We're going to drown!" (Luke 8:24). Jesus gets up, and Luke tells us that He rebukes the storm. In other words, He tells it to be quiet. Then He urges the disciples to stop their fear spiral, too, asking, "Where is your faith?" (verse 25).

Now, to recap, the disciples have just seen Jesus conquer the waters—one of their symbols of Chaos. Of course they're dumbfounded. They start asking one another if they have any concept of who this Man is: "Who is this? He commands even the winds and the water, and they obey him" (verse 25).

It's a really good question.

The reality is that storms speak. But the good news is that Jesus has muzzled both the Tempter and the tempest, which means you have the power to mute the Dragon when the chaos gets unbearable. Instead of entertaining lies, use the power at your disposal and put the muzzle back on the Dragon of deception.

The truth is, in this story the disciples' have a lot of faith—but it is fueling the wrong vehicle.

The issue is not their measure of faith but the misplacement of it.

Where is their faith? It's obvious, actually. Examine their words: "Master, Master, we're going to drown!" (verse

24). They believe in the power of the storm more than they believe in Jesus.

Their faith is in the storm. Their faith is in the new, re-branded Baal, the storm god.

Because the storm can never get your worship without first getting your faith. And the storm can't get your faith without getting your attention and your focus.

Where should their faith be? In the words spoken by Jesus. Before the storm comes, Jesus makes sure to speak to the disciples, and that should be the anchor to their faith. Jesus says in verse 22, "Let us go over to the other side of the lake." Those aren't simply directions. Embedded in them is a promise.

Jesus says that the destination is the other side of the lake—which means the storm is lying when it tells me that my journey will end at the bottom of the sea.

But unless that storm is muzzled—man, it can be convincing.

A moment of weakness. A moment of doubt.
When you're tired. When you're overwhelmed.
Like a skillful hunter stalks its prey, the Beast watches
    and waits.

On my own journey to conquering chaos, I've learned that sometimes it's simple to *obtain* order. But it is always difficult to *maintain* order. Because every time you choose order over chaos, the Beast leaves you alone and simply waits for an opportune time. There is no once-and-for-all test that God will give any of us to secure permanent order in our lives.

So, once we have some kind of order, the hard part is to keep it. Do you ever wish for that once-and-for-all test that doesn't exist? The kind of test where, once we pass it, everything is okay? That's not what God's offering us. He's offering us a thousand chances to let Him speak stillness into our storms. He's offering us the opportunity to grow in faith and to look to Him in everything, no matter how intense the storms become.

Reflect

Where is your faith currently placed—in the storm or in Jesus's promises? What would it look like to shift your focus?

_____

_____

_____

_____

When has Jesus muzzled a storm in your life? How did that experience change your trust in Him?

_____

_____

_____

_____

Pray

In prayer, ask God to rebuke or muzzle the voice of the Dragon in your heart.

Walking on Water
CHAPTER 24

> "Lord, if it's you," Peter replied, "tell me to come to you on the water."
>
> "Come," he said.
>
> Then Peter got down out of the boat, walked on the water and came toward Jesus. But when he saw the wind, he was afraid and, beginning to sink, cried out, "Lord, save me!"
>
> Immediately Jesus reached out his hand and caught him. "You of little faith," he said, "why did you doubt?"
>
> —MATTHEW 14:28–31

This final week offers us the opportunity to watch how Jesus confronted chaos, convincing the people closest to Him that He really was the Chaos-crushing God from their earliest stories. Today's story depicts the paradox of Jesus's humanity and divinity, and it shows how an encounter with the Chaos crusher helps us grow, even through our failures. It shows Jesus, who was fully human, spurring another human, Peter, to greater hope and faith.

Reread the story behind today's passage if you need to, starting in verse 25. The disciples see Jesus walking toward their boat, over the waves. It's windy out there on the deep waters. (Your Chaos-cycle sensor should be blaring right now.) Peter calls out to Him, and Jesus responds, telling Peter to walk on the waves with Him. Then . . . Peter sinks. But my point here is that he walks on the water for a moment. We need Jesus—the Man—to help us reach outside the Chaos cycle. What does Peter say? "Tell me to come to you on the water." Humans are inspired by other humans.

People have a phenomenally strong impact on one another. Here's an example from the sports world: As soon as Roger Bannister broke an "impossible" barrier by running a mile in under four minutes, it was as if every human on the planet received access to that iOS update. We're oddly interconnected and interdependent in that way.

Which explains how Peter can conquer the Chaos and walk on the Sea of Galilee, as Matthew's gospel details. Peter sees Jesus do it and therefore knows it is possible.

Maybe the image of Jesus overcoming the Chaos doesn't move you or inspire you. I can understand that point of view. And honestly, I'd say we're in the same boat. (Get it? I couldn't resist.) Jesus walking on the water has never been my favorite part of the story. Jesus walking on the water is incredible and highlights His divinity for me in a special way. But it's hard to see Jesus the way Peter saw Him.

Peter and all the disciples engaged Jesus as a human and needed a revelation of His divinity. Even when they realized He was the Jewish Messiah, that wasn't a divine category for them. The disciples didn't fully realize Jesus was divine until after the Resurrection.

However, most of us have engaged with Jesus as a divine being for all our Christian lives. We sing worship songs to Jesus. We pray to Him. We know Jesus as God, and therefore, we need the exact opposite revelation as the disciples did. Many of us desperately need a revelation of Jesus's humanity that will cause us to behold Jesus the Man, follow in His footsteps, and finally walk on our Chaos.

The Gospels can give us a starting point for this revelation. Read today's verses and other passages from these four books closely: What does Jesus say and do? Does anything surprise or confuse you? Does anything strike you as strange? Lean into those feelings and observations.

Since Jesus was here in the flesh, there's something so beautiful and personal about the stories described in the Gospels. But perhaps that doesn't quite cut it for you. Maybe you need a different angle to understand the human element of Jesus.

When you read today's passage about walking on the

water, maybe focus on Peter instead of on Jesus. Matthew, Mark, and John all include this story in their gospel narratives, but only Matthew adds the detail that Peter walked on the water too. And to be honest, it's my favorite part of the story. I may not be able to follow in Jesus's footsteps, but I for sure think I could walk in Peter's. Because Peter isn't divine at all. Much like Roger Bannister, Peter is the proof of what humans are capable of when they redefine what it means to be human and offer themselves to the Spirit of the living God. Peter is just as human as you and I are, and he walked on the Chaos.

What chaos is happening in your life right now? What kind of storm? Envision Jesus walking over that storm toward you. How do you feel when He tells you to "come"?

If you're anything like me, you're afraid to get out of the boat. After all, chaos has been having its way in your life, and it's made things difficult and messy for you. But don't look down at the waves—look at Jesus. He's walking over the chaos. Through His strength, it is possible for you to walk over it too. He's spurring you on to greater faith, hope, and love. And as you look at Him, listen to His voice—a voice that belongs to Someone who was fully human and who is calling us to become fully human too. That's why Peter got out of the boat; he trusted in the voice that was calling him.

And if Peter can conquer the Chaos, you can definitely conquer the chaos that exists in your life, whatever it is. It doesn't have the final word or the last laugh.

Reflect

What chaos is Jesus calling you to walk through with Him? What keeps you in the boat?

_____

_____

_____

_____

How does seeing Jesus's humanity help you believe He understands your struggles? What comfort do you find in this?

_____

_____

_____

_____

Pray

In prayer, ask God to reveal Himself to you in the person of Christ—both His divinity and His humanity.

Jonah
CHAPTER 25

> He answered, "A wicked and adulterous
> generation asks for a sign! But none will
> be given it except the sign of the prophet
> Jonah. For as Jonah was three days and
> three nights in the belly of a huge fish, so
> the Son of Man will be three days and
> three nights in the heart of the earth."
>
> —MATTHEW 12:39–40

Sometimes, Jesus can't say it any plainer. We just have to ask for faith to understand. A repeated pattern you'll find in the Gospels is Jesus trying to describe His Chaos-crushing plan to the disciples or a different audience and no one understanding Him. In today's verses, He tells some religious leaders that He's going to spend "three days and three nights in the heart of the earth." Admittedly, that one is easier to see from our side of history. He was talking about His own death, but the disciples would have to see it to believe it. Really, we can't blame them. It's hard for us to see what's right in front of us too.

There is a lot about Scripture that is difficult to accept. In some ways, it's easier to believe in claims that disprove the Bible than to accept the difficulties of really believing it and live like it's true. One accusation most often leveled against Scripture is that it's inconsistent. So, let's dive into one of those inconsistencies and feel it out together. But first, we need to look at some relevant context. If this feels like a left turn, just know that I'll bring it back around.

Here's a snippet from one of my favorite myths: The world of Greek mythology was full of a rich diversity of sea monsters, but none more important than Cetus (κῆτος or *Kētos* in Greek). Cetus makes an appearance in the famous myth of Perseus and Andromeda. To avoid total annihilation, an oracle instructed the king and queen of Aethiopia to sacrifice their daughter, Androm-eda, to the sea monster Cetus by tying her to a rock close to the shore. Nice, warm, loving family story, right? It was certainly popular, though, and it was told all over the ancient world.

But perhaps the most shocking place that I've seen this myth appear is on the lips of Jesus of Nazareth as He's debating some Pharisees in Matthew's gospel. In today's passage, Jesus uses the Greek word *kētos* (or κῆτος)* to describe whatever swallowed Jonah. Why most English

* *A Greek-English Lexicon of the New Testament,* trans. Joseph Henry Thayer (New York: Harper & Brothers, 1889), s.v. "*kētos*."

translations use the word "fish" here is mind-boggling to me. Because *kētos* ("latinized as cetus")* ain't a fish. Jesus clearly articulates that Jonah was in the belly of a sea monster or Chaos dragon.

But here's the thing: Jonah 1:17 just says the prophet was in a "huge fish." Not a dragon. Not a sea monster. A huge fish. So why does Jesus call this same fish a cetus?

When Western readers find inconsistencies like this, it typically triggers us to doubt the validity of the biblical text. Eastern readers are triggered by these wrinkles in the text as well—but triggered to solve the text's mysteries. Eastern (and ancient) readers believe that inconsistencies lead us from shallow water into the depths of wisdom, mystery, and paradox.

An Eastern approach to Scripture embraces the reality that God has hidden and concealed wisdom within His Word and that noticeable wrinkles in the text should trigger us to search matters out until no stone has been left unturned. Proverbs 25:2 teaches us, "It is the glory of God to conceal a matter; to search out a matter is the glory of kings." This proverb is the epitome of Eastern culture and an Eastern worldview.

Have you ever doubted the Bible because of its inconsistencies? Mysteries, paradoxes, and even seeming gaps are invitations to look closer. Yet how does this explana-

---

* *World History Encyclopedia,* s.v. "Sea Monster Ketos (Cetus)," December 17, 2014, www.worldhistory.org/image/3363/sea-monster-ketos -cetus/#google_vignette.

tion sit with you? Do mysteries incite you to fear or wonder?

If mysteries stir up fear in you, I just want you to know that you're not alone. A large contingent of us would like things to just make sense the first time, please. But that's not how life really is, is it? An uncomplicated, easy Bible couldn't reveal reality.

Let's go back to the mystery at hand: the "sign of the prophet Jonah" and the Greek mythology monster that Jesus promises to the crowd.

Jonah sinks to the bottom of the *tehom*. Is swallowed up by Chaos. Calls the belly of the beast the realm of the dead—aka his tomb. But then the belly of the beast is revealed to be a womb instead of a tomb.

And thus, Jonah is reborn.

This is what Jesus saw. This is what Matthew 12 is about. Once again, Jesus is claiming His title as Crusher of Chaos, hinting at the way He's going to overcome the ultimate Chaos—that of death. Jesus was saying not only that He would surrender Himself to the belly of the Beast but also that death wouldn't get the last laugh.

Which is why He used Jonah's story to predict that His tomb would also be a womb—and that from His resurrection, new-creation life would enter the world.

Do you see what He's doing here? The depth of the parallel between Jonah and Jesus wouldn't be possible without some initial confusion. Through paradox, mystery, and seeming inconsistency, God reveals Himself to us.

How incredible is that?

Reflect

How do you typically respond to mysteries in Scripture—
with fear or wonder? What shapes your response?

_____

_____

_____

_____

When has God used something confusing in your life to
reveal deeper truth? What did you learn through that
process?

_____

_____

_____

_____

Pray

In prayer, thank God for His willingness to reveal Himself
through mysteries.

Beginning Again
CHAPTER 26

> In the beginning was the Word, and the
> Word was with God, and the Word was
> God. He was with God in the beginning.
> Through him all things were made; without
> him nothing was made that has been
> made. In him was life, and that life was the
> light of all mankind. The light shines in the
> darkness, and the darkness has not
> overcome it.
>
> —JOHN 1:1–5

Maybe you've already noticed this, but the New Testament builds on the Old Testament—the new covenant doesn't get rid of the old one. If anything, it refines and deepens it. Think of it this way: It's the same song set to a new variation—one that adds meaning to the first version instead of completely eclipsing it.

Nowhere is this clearer than in the gospel of John, the last gospel to be written and, it could be argued, the strangest. When John sees Jesus, it's like he's seeing the book of Genesis in human form. John is obsessed with two things: Jesus and Genesis. So, when we read John's gospel, we get a glimpse of the Messiah as this disciple saw Him—through the lens of Genesis.

John starts his gospel account with some iconic words: "In the beginning" (1:1). Does that sound familiar? With the amount of time we've spent on the first verses of the Bible, I certainly hope so.

In. The. Beginning. Talk about bold.

John is making it very clear right away that he is writing a new Genesis.

I think it's difficult for us to comprehend how daring it was for John to begin his account with these three words. It was unheard of for a Jewish author to attempt to appropriate the venerated opening words of the Torah. John's got some serious chutzpah, and he sees in the person of Jesus the same creative power that formed the universe.

We've studied the original creation account in Genesis extensively these past few weeks so we can truly appreciate the depth and nuances of the remix: the new creation story that John gives us in his gospel account. Let's compare them for ourselves, just from the first few lines of each book. Here's the beginning of Genesis again. (I know, we've been here a lot, but bear with me.)

In the beginning God created the heavens and the earth. Now the earth was formless and empty, darkness was over the surface of the deep, and the Spirit of God was hovering over the waters. (Genesis 1:1–2)

Okay, pop quiz time. What was God doing on the first day of creation? Need a clue? Check the final sentence of the verses we're reading today from John 1.

The first day of creation is God separating *light from darkness*. What does John say in his first lines about Jesus? "The light shines in the darkness, and the darkness has not overcome it." The parallel hits you upside the head once you can see it, doesn't it? It was there all along.

"The Word was with God" (John 1:1), and "the Spirit of God was hovering over the waters" (Genesis 1:2). The two accounts, taken together, reveal to us *how* the world was created: through the bond of love shared between the three persons present—Father, Son, and Spirit.

Genesis is a story of God conquering Chaos and creating Order in the cosmos.

Which means the new Genesis is probably about Chaos and Order as well.

I would contend that John believes everything about Jesus: His teaching and His miracles. His birth. His life. His death. His resurrection. Everything. That it has all brought new creation into this broken cosmos.

And now that the Holy Spirit dwells in us, we can finally get to the sixth and final stage of the Chaos cycle and demonstrate to the Lord that we can be tested and trusted. The resurrection of Jesus means the rules on the playing field have permanently changed.

In the new creation, we have a secret weapon. A secret weapon that made its appearance on the first day of the week as Mary went to a garden to anoint the body of Jesus. A secret weapon that raised the literal body of Christ and empowers the figurative body of Christ to

> conquer the Chaos,
> survive the waters,
> receive the Spirit,
> obey God's voice,
> embrace the Order,
> and pass the test.

This was the Jesus who John knew. The Jesus who brings new creation. The Jesus who conquers Chaos. The Jesus who cleanses us with His blood so we can receive the in-filling of the Holy Spirit. The Jesus who gives us a new beginning, breaks cycles, and teaches us to pass tests so we can sustain the Order that He's created.

The fact that John is basing his gospel on Genesis isn't just a cool parallel or an insight into Scripture. When Jesus comes into our hearts, He begins the work of re-creating them. Through the bond of love shared by the Father, Son, and Spirit, we can be renewed.

What in your life needs renewal?

Maybe it's an impossible relationship.

A difficult job.

A stubborn health problem—something that feels incurable.

The way you view yourself.

It could be anything. Or a lot of things.

Don't call whatever comes to your mind "big" or "small." God wants you to bring everything on your heart before Him. Bring all those things to God now, and lay them before Him. Ask Him to come into your heart and, through the love that created the world, make you new.

Reflect

What areas of your life need Christ's re-creating work? How have you seen Him bring new beginnings before?

_____

_____

_____

_____

Where do you need to trust God's ordering work in your current circumstances? What makes this trust challenging?

_____

_____

_____

_____

Pray

In prayer, thank God for making all things new in Christ.

Back to the Garden
CHAPTERS 27 AND 28

> Jesus, knowing all that was going to
> happen to him, went out and asked them,
> "Who is it you want?"
>
> "Jesus of Nazareth," they replied.
>
> "I am he," Jesus said. (And Judas the
> traitor was standing there with them.)
> When Jesus said, "I am he," they drew
> back and fell to the ground.
>
> —JOHN 18:4–6

There are more links to Genesis in John than I could cover in a book, let alone in these final days we're spending together. My goal here is to open your eyes to the parallel so that when you encounter the books of Genesis and John in other contexts—maybe at church, in your own study, or with a small group of other believers—you can look for the links and be amazed by them. But perhaps you'll indulge me while I give just one more example that specifically relates to the Chaos cycle:

Chaos.
Deep waters.
Wind or Spirit of God.
The voice of Yahweh.
Divine Order.
A failed test.
Repeat.

Today, we're headed to that final step: the failed test. Let me set the stage: John is picking up exactly where Genesis leaves off. He makes it abundantly clear that his gospel is riffing off Genesis, so if you're expecting John to focus on water—one of our primary symbols for Chaos and creation—I can promise that you won't be disappointed. Throughout the book of John, water takes center stage as a powerful and intentional symbol.

In John 2, we have six stone water jars used for ceremonial cleansing.
In John 3, Jesus tells Nicodemus he must be born of water and the Spirit.
In John 4, Jesus offers a Samaritan woman living water when He meets her at a well.
In John 5, we're at the Pool of Bethesda where angels periodically trouble the waters.

In John 6, Jesus walks on the water in the middle of a storm.

In John 7, Jesus says that rivers of living water will flow from those who believe in Him.

In John 9, we have blindness healed by Jesus's saliva and a visit to the Pool of Siloam.

In John 19, Jesus's side is pierced, bringing a sudden flow of blood and water.

So, let's recap. Humanity has descended into Chaos. And John shows us water—lots of water.

You'll have to take my word for it that the rest of the Chaos cycle is fulfilled within his pages. But before we get to the point I want to talk about—the test—I'll just mention the step preceding it: Order. Oh, we definitely have Order. John orders everything around the number seven. Can you remember where we've seen that number before? Yeah, in creation. Genesis 1.

In John's gospel there are seven miracles that John calls signs.

There are seven strategically placed discourses of teaching.

Jesus attends seven festivals throughout this account.

Jesus reveals His identity seven times, and each is marked by the words "I am."

And the book actually follows a seven-day structure.

Talk about intricate and ordered.

But John's gospel doesn't have a temptation narrative

where Jesus and Satan face off in the desert. John omits that entire part of Jesus's life. So, where's the moment of testing? My hunch is that John would place this moment of truth within a garden.

Let's remember what happened in the garden in Genesis. Adam and Eve succumbed to temptation and fear—they failed the test. Then, when God called to them, Adam answered, "I heard you in the garden, and I was afraid because I was naked; so I hid" (Genesis 3:10).

Now in John's gospel, just before Jesus is captured and crucified, He takes His disciples to a very specific place—a garden. Of course! Yet what does Jesus do instead of hiding in the garden when someone comes looking for him? As we see in our verses for today, He responds, "I am he."

Jesus owns His identity. He's stepping up to the plate instead of running away. He knows what's coming, and with His Chaos-crushing power, He's ready to take it on. If you need proof that this is a powerful moment, look at the final part of today's passage. Everyone in the garden *falls down*. Whoa.

But how did those guys get into the garden in the first place? One of Jesus's disciples, Judas, brought them there personally. Now, I'm going to try to shift slightly our perspective of Judas because I think his story shows what happens when we are tempted in the garden without the power of Christ behind us. Because Judas was in the garden that evening too—and he took the path that Adam and Eve had taken before him. He succumbed to the voice of the Dragon, just like they did. Just like our very first parents, Judas was unwilling to look at the larger picture because he believed so deeply in his own concerns.

What if Judas wasn't trying to get Jesus killed that night? We know that most, if not all, of the disciples believed that Jesus had come to be a political leader. Perhaps Judas thought he could orchestrate a scenario that would finally push Jesus over the edge and cause Him to rally the troops and start a violent revolution. Maybe Judas was manipulating the situation to get Jesus to react based on who he wanted Jesus to be as opposed to who Jesus was called to be. Maybe Judas had an agenda. And regardless of what Jesus had said, Judas simply could not let go of his agenda in exchange for the mission Jesus called them to follow.

In this way, there's a Judas in each of us. A part of us that would rather be loyal to our agendas than the mission God has called us to. Consider how Judas responded when his plan didn't work and Jesus was actually arrested. Judas was remorseful to the point of suicide.

This small passage in John helps us see how Jesus stepped up to the plate and passed the test. When we're tried, we often fail and hide like Adam or overreach like Judas. Instead, we'd do well to remember the words of Christ as He faced temptation: "I am he." Because He is.

Regardless of the particularities of our situations and temptations, these words of Jesus hold tremendous power for us. And as we trust Him and submit to His ways over ours, we'll watch as He crushes the chaos in our lives.

Reflect

In what ways do you relate to either Adam's hiding or Judas's manipulating? How is Jesus inviting you to choose a different response?

_____

_____

_____

_____

What would it mean for you to fully embrace your identity in Christ today? What holds you back?

_____

_____

_____

_____

Pray

In prayer, ask God for the humility to accept His plans and His ways over yours.

FINAL DAY—
DAY 30

THE SEED
MUST DIE
CHAPTER 29

Very truly I tell you, unless a kernel of
wheat falls to the ground and dies, it
remains only a single seed. But if it dies, it
produces many seeds. Anyone who loves
their life will lose it, while anyone who
hates their life in this world will keep it for
eternal life.

—JOHN 12:24–25

Thank you for spending this whole month with me and
the beauties of Genesis and the Gospels. I trust that this is
only the beginning. May you continue to see in the words
of Scripture these patterns and reiterations that reveal new
things about God and His desires for us.

It's our last day together, contemplating how Jesus crushes the chaos in our lives. We stopped in kind of an odd spot yesterday. Jesus withstands temptation and goes to the cross—but the ending is nothing like any of His followers expected.

After three years of successfully confronting the chaos of the Dragon throughout the Gospels, Jesus had only one form of chaos left to defeat. One final step in this epic journey to crush the Chaos and establish divine Order for the new creation.

Jesus has conquered the desert wilderness, overcome the temptation of the Beast, muzzled the Dragon, and tamed the raging storm. Jesus and Peter have both tread on the surface of the deep.

However, Chaos has not been fully crushed.

The Beast and the desert have been crushed. The flood and the storm, the *tannin* and the *tehom,* the wilderness and darkness—all crushed by Jesus.

Jesus has confronted and conquered almost every single symbol of Chaos that existed in the ancient world. Jesus is undefeated. Chaos has never gotten the best of Him. The Dragon has failed at every turn to tempt, overpower, or outwit Jesus. The odds are stacked in Jesus's favor as we approach the climax of the Gospels.

Every single piece of evidence pointed to the fact that Jesus of Nazareth would continue an undefeated streak of crushing Chaos, but then the chaos of death defeated Jesus on the cross.

As the Dragon and Chaos celebrated the death of Jesus,

they didn't realize that He was a seed. And the true power of a seed can be unlocked only when it dies. They buried Jesus in the earth, and the seed of the new creation was planted in the depth of the old creation.

That's the gospel. God planted a garden. Chaos replaced it with a wilderness. For three years of earthly ministry, Jesus worked tirelessly to landscape His Father's vineyard and restore the Order that had been lost and nearly forgotten. Then in a shocking turn of events, Chaos defeated the second Adam, the Gardener, on the cross as darkness and death prevailed. But in killing Jesus, Chaos planted the seed of new creation into the soil of this earth.

All of this was an odd and bewildering spot for the disciples, and you know what? It can be odd and bewildering for us too. If the story of Christ crushing chaos feels unfinished, that's because it is. This is the part where we step in—or, rather, where we let Him step in for us. Where we bring God the chaos in our lives and willingly give Him our whole selves, just like Jesus did.

Think about the very beginning of this month, when I asked you what chaos looked like in your life. In this final day together, I'm presenting what Jesus offers as the solution: surrendering ourselves completely.

God wants everything:

He wants you to tell Him about the chaos in your life and exactly how it has affected you.

He wants you to bring everything before Him, both good and bad.

He wants you to give Him every single relationship and responsibility, including the things you are grasping too tightly and the things that are weighing you down and that you wish would disappear.

He wants you to give Him your hopes and dreams for the future.

He wants the memories that keep you up at night.

He wants your fears and worries.

He wants your gifts and talents.

He wants the things that you've never been willing to give over to anyone else.

He wants you, all of you, completely.

And then He wants to help you bring that chaos into order—His Order.

Are you willing to yield all this to Him? Are you willing to accept His ways over yours? I pray that you are. I pray that I am too.

If we're going to be in His Order, then we have to go in sequence—the order described in today's verse: "unless a kernel of wheat falls to the ground and dies."

That's how God's Order works. Death to self *first*. Our first step is to surrender everything to Him completely. Then He brings about His Order. And you know what? The "single seed" that we give up to Him—that we lose—becomes a thousand new seeds.

Because that's what God does: He creates. He regenerates. He makes everything new. And if we're willing to begin over and over again, He will cultivate something new and beautiful through us. Something so wonderful that we couldn't dare even to imagine or hope for it for ourselves.

So, to ensure that we don't allow the chaos of life back into His garden, we die. We die to our old selves, to who we were, to the patterns and systems of the old earth. And we learn to rebuild our lives based on the blueprints and designs that the Gardener of our souls managed to recover.

We die to ourselves.

We enter the garden.

We learn the blueprints.

We maintain Order.

And we crush the Chaos.

Reflect

What are you most reluctant to surrender to God's ordering work? What makes this particularly difficult?

_____

_____

_____

_____

How has your understanding of chaos and order changed through this study? What new hope do you have for God's work in your life?

_____

_____

_____

_____

Pray

In prayer, present yourself to God, praying the words of Jesus: "Anyone who loves their life will lose it."

MANNY ARANGO is a Bible nerd and founder of ARMA Courses—an online educational platform that helps Christians become biblically literate. The platform has grown to thousands of monthly subscribers since launching in 2020.

Born in Boston, Massachusetts, Manny was a teaching pastor at Social Dallas under pastors Robert and Taylor Madu and is now the lead pastor, along with his wife, Tia, of The Garden in Houston, Texas. He graduated from Northern Seminary in June 2024 with a doctorate in New Testament studies.

Manny has been married to his beautiful wife for more than a decade, and they have a son named Theophilus.

Instagram: @mannyarango

TikTok: @manny_arango

Also from author and pastor
MANNY ARANGO

A deeply biblical and fresh look at how an ancient reading of the Bible leads to lasting peace, inviting followers of Jesus to join Him in bringing order to the chaos of their lives and the world.

In this compelling companion guide to the book *Crushing Chaos*, engage with key questions, dig into the Bible, and complete activities that will help you chart a path through the chaos to a life of order, joy, and peace.

WATERBROOK

Learn more about Manny Arango's books at
waterbrookmultnomah.com.

01 14